FINANCING
AMERICAN
RELIGION

For Fred Hofheinz. MC

To Judy and Susan, who left too soon. SLM

Financing
American
Religion

EDITED BY MARK CHAVES &
SHARON L. MILLER

A Division of
ROWMAN & LITTLEFIELD PUBLISHERS, INC.
Lanham • New York • Toronto • Plymouth, UK

ALTAMIRA PRESS
A division of Rowman & Littlefield Publishers, Inc.
A wholly owned subsidary of The Rowman & Littlefield Publishing Group, Inc.
4501 Forbes Boulevard, Suite 200
Lanham, MD 20706
www.altamirapress.com

Estover Road
Plymouth PL6 7PY
United Kingdom

British Library Cataloguing in Publication Information Available

The previous edition of this book was previously cataloged by the Library of Congress as
follows:

Financing American religion / edited by Mark Chaves and Sharon L. Miller.
    p. cm.
  Includes bibliographical references and index.
  ISBN-13: 978-0-7619-9036-9 (alk. paper)
  ISBN-10: 0-7619-9036-4 (alk. paper)
  ISBN-13: 978-0-7619-9037-6 (pbk. : alk. paper)
  ISBN-10: 0-7619-9037-2 (pbk. : alk. paper)
  1. Christian giving. I. Chaves, Mark. II. Miller, Sharon L.
  BV772 F47 1998
  262'.0068'1—ddc21   98-25448

Printed in the United States of America

♾™ The paper used in this publication meets the minimum requirements of American
National Standard for Information Sciences—Permanence of Paper for Printed Library
Materials, ANSI/NISO Z39.48–1992.

Contents

PART IV. CONCLUSION

Preface

This book emerges from an evaluation of the Lilly Endowment Inc.'s Financing American Religion initiative. Early in this evaluation project, it became clear that the Endowment, through this grantmaking initiative, had sponsored the creation of a body of knowledge about religion and money, and it had fostered a community of scholars and practitioners focused on the complex connections between religion and money. To evaluate this body of work meant to be in the privileged position of seeing virtually all the cutting-edge work on this subject as it was being produced, before much of it was published. It meant being able to assess the state of knowledge in an area both of considerable interest to scholars and of considerable concern to those who care about religious organizations in the United States.

This volume is, first and foremost, an effort to share the experience of seeing in one place all the pieces of knowledge generated by the Endowment's initiative on the financing of American religion. Some of the chapters come from published works that are, by now, well known. Other chapters have appeared previously only in difficult-to-find pamphlets. Each individual part had its own life prior to this volume, but it was rare for any of these pieces to be seen in relation to other pieces. Moreover, it seems unlikely that anyone other than Lilly Endowment program staff ever saw *all* this work together in one place and thereby discerned the full contours of our knowledge on financing American religion. Putting these pieces together, side by side, enables readers to benefit from, and critically assess, this body of work qua a body of work. Readers will be able to see which results and patterns reoccur, which issues from a particular study are echoed in other studies, and which holes remain in our knowledge. This volume was assembled, and is offered, with the conviction that the whole created by these chapters is greater than the sum of the parts.

This volume is organized into four parts. Part I contains eight chapters focused mainly on individual giving to religious congregations. Some of these chapters report on the contemporary scene, others are historical; some are based on surveys, others on archival material, still others on in-depth interviews. Together, these chapters present an overview of what is currently known about the social, historical, economic, and cultural aspects of giving to religious congregations.

Part II shifts from the perspective of the individual who gives money to the perspective of the congregation receiving and managing that money. The three chapters in this section report financial and other data from a national survey of congregations, analyze certain key characteristics of congregations with substantial endowments, and assess the capacity and willingness of clergy to manage their congregations' material resources.

Part III continues the focus on organizations, but shifts attention to the financing of religious organizations other than congregations. There are chapters here on Catholic schools, theological schools, parachurch organizations, and religious nonprofit organizations. Part IV contains two essays, each of which reflects on this body of work as a whole.

A central goal of the Endowment's financing initiative was to generate knowledge that would be useful to those who lead religious institutions in the United States. Rigorous research is not always useful research, and true knowledge is not always practical knowledge. Several features of this book are intended to help close the common gap between research results and useful knowledge. The chapters are short, presenting key results with minimum methodological detail. We have tried to include methodological information sufficient for readers to assess for themselves the meaning, generalizability, and value of the findings, but we probably have erred on the side of sparseness. Each chapter, however, contains a complete citation to the larger work from which the chapter in this book is adapted.

Most important, each chapter in the book's first three sections ends with a set of practical conclusions. Some of these conclusions are more practical than others. Some call for fairly specific kinds of action; others call for subtle shifts in understanding. All of these conclusions, at the very least, ought to help religious leaders and others understand a bit better some aspect of the material situation their organizations face. This is not a "how-to" book; it is, however, a book intended to bridge somewhat the chasm between research and practice, between scholarship and organizational leadership. The practical conclusions at the end of each chapter are offered in that spirit.

Although there was more good work funded through the Lilly Endowment's financing initiative than could be included in this volume, all of the research underlying the chapters in this book was supported via this initiative. I think it is safe to say that neither this body of work nor the community of scholars and practitioners who have produced it would have existed were it not for the vision of Fred Hofheinz, the Endowment Program Officer spearheading the financing initiative, and Craig Dykstra, Vice President of the Endowment's Religion Division. I know that this volume would not have existed were it not for Bob Lynn's visit to me in the spring of 1995 to persuade me to take on the challenge of evaluating this initiative, Fred Hofheinz's guidance and unwavering support and encouragement through the course of this project, and Kathleen Cahalan's skillful and graceful tutoring—over the course of 18 months—on just what it means to evaluate an Endowment initiative. Sharon Miller began this project as an appreciated graduate assistant; she ends it as a valued colleague and full partner in the editing of this book.

Most of the work preparing this volume occurred under the auspices of DePaul University's Center for Applied Social Research. Special thanks are due David Nygren, Miriam Ukeritis, Jane Halpert, and George Michel for providing a supportive environment for this project and for me.

Mark Chaves
Department of Sociology
University of Arizona

PART **I**

INDIVIDUAL GIVING

Chapter 1

Giving in Five Denominations

DEAN R. HOGE
CHARLES ZECH
PATRICK McNAMARA
MICHAEL J. DONAHUE

More donations go to churches than to any other single type of organization in American society. *Giving USA* (1995:85) estimated religious giving at $58.8 billion, or 45 percent of all giving by individuals and organizations in 1994. Others have estimated religious giving to be as high as 63 percent of all philanthropic giving (Hodgkinson and Weitzman 1992:38). Relatedly, American religion depends on individual giving more than on any other source of material resources. Our own research, on which this chapter is based, finds that congregations, on average, receive about 90 percent of their funds from individuals' donations. American religion and individual giving are thus inextricably entwined. Seeking to understand the determinants of religious giving is simultaneously seeking to understand both the material basis of American churches and a significant chunk of the overall donative behavior of individuals in our society.

AUTHORS' NOTE: This chapter is adapted from our book, *Money Matters: Personal Giving in American Churches*, 1996, © Westminster John Knox Press; used with permission. Readers interested in more details about either our methods or our results should consult that volume.

To investigate the determinants of religious giving, we drew random samples of 125 congregations in each of five denominations: the Assemblies of God, the Southern Baptist Convention, the Roman Catholic Church, the Evangelical Lutheran Church in America, and the Presbyterian Church (U.S.A). Field workers visited these congregations and, working together with pastors, completed a congregational profile. We also mailed a questionnaire to a random sample of 30 members from each selected congregation. Data collection occurred in 1993. Our congregational response rate was 84.8 percent; our member questionnaire response rate was 61.2 percent. The findings reported here are based on 625 congregational profiles and 10,902 individual questionnaires returned by members.[1] Our membership sample, however, is disproportionately composed of the most loyal and active members, and readers should interpret results accordingly.

FINDINGS

Basic Facts. Other studies have shown that the level of giving to churches varies greatly across denominations. The percentage of household income given by church members varies as much as fivefold across denominations. Figure 1.1 presents the mean percentage of income contributed for each of 23 denominations. Latter-Day Saints (Mormons) head the list with over 7 percent. Lutherans and Catholics are near the bottom, giving, on average, a little more than 1 percent. Almost half of the denominations range from 2 to 3 percent.

The amounts given by church members in any congregation vary widely. All research shows that a minority of members give the most money. As a rule of thumb, 75 percent of the money in a typical church is given by 25 percent of the people. Sometimes the ratio is closer to 80:20. This skewness in giving is not unique to churches; a similar pattern exists in nonreligious member organizations as well, and Chapter 4 in this volume explains why. Here, however, this pattern relates to an important fact about denominational differences in giving levels: Denominational differences are generated almost completely by the top fifth of the givers in each denomination. That is, if we looked only at the bottom 80 percent of givers in each denomination, there would be much smaller differences in average giving across denominations.

---

1   We still have 625 congregational profiles even with a response rate below 100 percent because we replaced refusing congregations with similar ones until achieving our goal of 125 congregations per denomination.

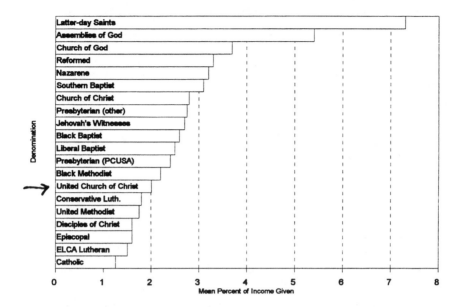

Figure 1.1. Giving as a Percentage of Income

NOTE: This figure is based on analysis by Stephen Hart. The data are from the *General Social Survey,* *1987-1989* (Davis and Smith 1994), and include persons who attend religious services at least yearly.

Only when we compare the most generous 20 percent of members do large denominational differences emerge.

Table 1.1 compares giving in our five denominations in terms of absolute dollars rather than percentage of income. Three different estimates of individual giving are presented. The individual giving estimates in the top line of the table are drawn from our congregational profiles and are calculated by dividing each congregation's total receipts from giving by the number of regular attenders in that congregation. The giving estimates in the second line of the table also are drawn from the congregational profiles, this time dividing the same numerator—giving receipts—by the number of households reported for that congregation. The estimates in the bottom line of the table are drawn from our individual questionnaire and represent members' self-reports of their own household giving to their congregations. There are many things that might be observed about this table; here we emphasize four points. First, comparing the second and third lines in the table, the giving levels that are based on individual self-reports are much higher than those estimated by dividing congregational receipts by households. There likely is

TABLE 1.1 Three Estimates of Average Annual Household Contributions (in U.S. dollars)

	Assemblies of God	Baptist	Catholic	Lutheran	Presbyterian
Total congregational receipts from giving divided by the number of attenders	877	952	283	824	1,106
Total congregational receipts from giving divided by the number of households	1,696	1,154	386	746	1,085
Self-reported household contributions	3,254	2,810	1,032	1,471	2,036

some inflation in self-reported giving, but we interpret this difference as largely reflecting the fact that our lay sample disproportionately contains the most active and loyal—and therefore the most generous—givers.

Second, comparing the first two lines in the table, dividing total receipts by the number of households in a congregation produces about the same giving estimate as does dividing by the number of regular attenders *except* for the Assemblies of God. In that denomination, estimated per household giving is almost double the estimate for per attender giving, whereas in no other denomination is one of these numbers more than one-third larger than the other number. This means that, whereas in the other four denominations the number of households reported by clergy is about the same as the number of regular attenders, Assemblies of God clergy reported only about half as many households in their congregations as there are regular attenders, suggesting that Assemblies congregations have more attenders per household than do the other denominations.

Third, there are substantial differences among denominations in average giving levels. Using the second line of the table—average household contributions calculated from congregational reports—Assemblies households are most generous, followed by Baptists, Presbyterians, Lutherans, and Catholics, in that order. Note that this same rank ordering is evident in Figure 1.1, which portrays giving as a percentage of income and is derived from a national sample of individuals.

Fourth, consistent with previous research (especially Greeley and McManus 1987), Catholic giving is substantially below Protestant giving on both estimates.

Explaining Giving. Because it has long been observed that Catholic giving is lower than Protestant giving, we devoted substantial attention to investigating the sources of this difference. Here are eight of our key findings, the first six of which concern the absence of evidence for factors widely believed to be responsible for low levels of Catholic giving relative to Protestants.

1. It is *not true* that Catholic giving is lower than Protestant giving because Catholic churches are larger on average than Protestant churches. Catholic churches are, indeed, much larger than Protestant congregations—in our data more than eight times as large—but we did not find a consistent relationship between congregational size and giving levels.

2. It is *not true* that Catholic giving is lower than Protestant giving because Catholics are angrier than Protestants with their denominational leaders. Catholics are no more angry with denominational leaders than members of the other four denominations are angry at their leaders.

3. It is *not true* that Catholic giving is lower than Protestant giving because Catholics give more than Protestants to nonparish denominational organizations. Catholic giving to nonparish Catholic causes is no higher than its equivalent in the other four denominations.

4. It is *not true* that Catholic giving is lower than Protestant giving because Catholics are more likely to send their children to religious schools. It is true that Catholics are more likely than Protestants to have their children in parochial schools, but families with children in Catholic schools do not give a smaller amount to their churches than other families of the same age.

5. It is *not true* that Catholic giving is lower than Protestant giving because Catholic parishes are less democratic in decision making. Democracy in itself is not a predictor of giving in any of our denominations.

6. It is *not true* that Catholic giving is lower than Protestant giving because Catholics are less convinced that their parish or denomination has serious financial needs. In our study, Catholic laity are no less convinced than others that their parish or their denomination has serious needs.

7. It *is true* that Catholic giving is lower partially because Catholic parishes emphasize stewardship and individual giving less than Protestant churches. We found that a substantial percentage of Catholic parishioners do not even know whether or not their parish has such an emphasis.

8. It *is true* that Catholic giving is lower partially because Catholic parishes are less likely to use pledge cards for members to indicate in writing what they intend to give in the coming year.

This effort to explain Protestant versus Catholic differences notwithstanding, in our opinion the findings of greatest practical usefulness are those that pertain *within* denominations. Because church leaders in each denomination operate within a more or less given institutional and theological context, comparing different denominations to each other is less practically useful. Pastors will say, "But we're not Pentecostals. We're not Mormons. We're who we are, and we have come to this point after years of prayer and experience." They are right. For this reason, we focus now on determinants of individual giving that pertain within each of the five denominations that we studied. Because these factors emerge as important within each of five very different institutional and theological contexts, they are likely to be more generally applicable across the religious spectrum.

Three factors in particular overwhelmingly and consistently are associated with higher levels of giving within each of the denominations that we studied.[2] First, consistent with past research on giving of all sorts, the level of family income greatly influences giving to congregations. In all denominations, members with low income levels give at similar (low) rates, and the amount given goes up with income. Giving goes up faster in some denominations than in others, a finding that adds additional nuance to the observation we made earlier that denominational differences in giving mainly represent differences among the most generous givers. That is, it seems that denominational differences in giving mainly reflect different giving habits of their highest income members.

Second, members who are actively involved in congregational life give more. Both church attendance and hours spent volunteering for church work are highly predictive of giving. In the four Protestant denominations that we studied, members who were in church more than once a week gave between one-quarter and one-half times more even than members who were in church about once a week. For Catholics, those in church about once a week gave more than twice as much as those in church two or three times a month.

Third, members who plan their giving by the year or by the month give more than those who decide week by week. Persons who say they give 10 percent or more of their income of course give the most. In general, however, those who decide to give a certain percentage of their income annually— even if they decide on less than 10 percent—give more than those who decide on an annual dollar amount. Furthermore, those who decide on either a

---

2   Some parts of our results suggest that two other factors—small congregational size and traditionalist theology—may be related to higher levels of individual giving, but the patterns are inconsistent across denominations.

percentage of income or a dollar amount to be given in the next year give much more than those who decide on a weekly amount or decide week by week. Planned giving, then, produces more generosity than does spontaneous giving.

Of the many factors that do *not* explain individual differences in giving, one is particularly important to mention because it is widely believed to be important. We refer here to the notion that individual giving responds to denominational policies and actions. Church officials tend to think, for example, that Presbyterian unhappiness over the 1993 Re-Imagining Conference (criticized as radical and heretical by many in the church) has taken a toll in Presbyterian giving, or that Baptist unhappiness with the power struggles at the national level has taken a toll in Baptist giving. Yet we could find no evidence that attitudes about denominational leadership affect giving to the local church. All our findings indicate that giving is felt to be a matter between the church member and God or between the member and his or her congregation. It is an open question whether happiness or unhappiness with denominational leadership affects *allocation* decisions in churches—how much money congregations send to denominations versus how much they send elsewhere or spend locally. Whatever the effect on congregational decisions, these feelings have no noticeable effect on the amount given to congregations by individuals.

PRACTICAL CONCLUSIONS

Our results suggest several conclusions that should be of interest to those who care in a practical way about individuals' giving to congregations.

1. Individual giving is one aspect of congregational involvement in general and probably should not be treated—either in theory or in practice—in isolation from that broader context. People who are more involved will give more; attempting to increase giving without increasing involvement will be difficult.   *hours of worship Type church*

2. Giving is higher when it is institutionalized rather than spontaneous. Tying giving to a percentage of income and using annual pledge cards both seem to increase individual giving.

3. Giving is far more responsive to local conditions—family income and congregational practices—than to nonlocal, denominational conditions. If giving is to be affected, it will be affected through local change rather than through regional or national change.

4. Denominational differences in giving to congregations mainly reflect differences among the most generous givers and among the highest income members. These are the members whose financial situations and giving habits provide the most room for variation. They might also be the members whose giving habits are most amenable to change.

REFERENCES

Davis, James A., and Tom W. Smith. 1994. *General Social Surveys, 1972-1994* [machine-readable data file]. Chicago: National Opinion Research Center.

Giving USA. 1995. New York: American Association of Fund-Raising Counsel Trust for Philanthropy.

Greeley, Andrew, and William McManus. 1987. *Catholic Contributions: Sociology and Policy.* Chicago: Thomas More Press.

Hodgkinson, Virginia A., and Murray S. Weitzman. 1992. *Giving and Volunteering in the United States.* Washington, DC: Independent Sector.

Chapter **2**

Basic Trends in Religious Giving

1921-1995

JOHN RONSVALLE
SYLVIA RONSVALLE

What trends can be identified throughout this century in the level of financial support members have given their churches? This chapter relies on official membership and financial data collected by many denominations to provide a basic overview of trends in religious giving in the United States. The data were obtained by national or regional denominational offices that ask each congregation to provide membership and financial data. The National Council of the Churches of Christ in the U.S.A. compiles and publishes these denominational data in its annual report, *Yearbook of American and Canadian Churches* (YACC). The analyses reported here use these YACC data, sometimes supplementing them with data obtained directly from denominational offices.

Two sets of denominational data have been analyzed. First, a group of 29 Protestant denominations has provided comparable data to the *YACC* since 1968. The comparison begins in 1968 because, starting that year, a consistent distinction was made in the *YACC* between each denomination's "full" or "confirmed" members, on the one hand, and "inclusive" membership, on the other hand. The 29 denominations that provided data throughout this period represent just over 100,000 congregations and include 30 million full or confirmed members. As a basis of comparison, it has been estimated there are approximately 350,000 religious congregations of any type in the United States (Hodgkinson and Weitzman 1992:116).

It should be noted that, while the 29 denominations span a broad theological spectrum of the Protestant church, the Roman Catholic Church and major African American communions have not consistently published financial data and so are not included in this set. However, as will be seen, available survey-based financial data for the Roman Catholic Church suggest trends in the same direction as those for this group of 29 denominations. Also, The United Methodist Church was formed by merger in 1969, and 1968 data were not available for The Episcopal Church; therefore, neither of these denominations is included in this data set. Data that will be reviewed in this chapter indicate that trends in The United Methodist Church, the second largest Protestant denomination in the United States, are similar to those in the 29 denominations.

The second set includes data for 11 Protestant denominations, and their historical precursors, that have reported data in a fairly consistent fashion between 1921 and 1995. This group includes nine denominations from the 29-denomination data set: eight mainline Protestant denominations and the Southern Baptist Convention. Here, both The United Methodist Church and The Episcopal Church are included as well, with averages used for missing years over this longer time line. It should be noted that composite figures provided by the source material are used prior to 1953 in the 1921-1995 comparison; this series should be viewed as providing a general sense of patterns throughout the century.

These two series are used to present a descriptive overview of trends in per member giving. The 29-denomination data set also is used to review the levels of giving directed by congregational leadership to local operations versus "benevolences." Benevolences include international missions as well as national and local charities. Benevolences also include support of denominational organizations themselves, including national and regional offices, as well as seminaries and schools, and interdenominational organizations supported by the denomination.

A comparison between giving in eight denominations affiliated with the National Council of the Churches of Christ in the U.S.A. (NCC) and giving in eight denominations associated with the National Association of Evangelicals (NAE) explores patterns in two specific subsections of the theological spectrum. Finally, a preliminary analysis that explores the relationship of giving and membership is presented. Readers interested in additional methodological and empirical details should consult the latest in the annual series of reports, *The State of Church Giving* (Ronsvalle and Ronsvalle 1997).

FINDINGS

Donations and Income in Inflation-Adjusted Dollars. The calculation of giving as a percentage of income is based on three factors: the amount of dollars donated, the number of members, and U.S. per capita disposable (after-tax) personal income. The dollars donated can be considered in current dollars, which indicates the value of the dollar in the year it was donated or earned. They can also be considered in inflation-adjusted, or "real" dollars. The "current" versus "real" distinction is not relevant for giving as a percentage of income: As long as one uses current or inflation-adjusted dollars for both donations and income, the proportions will be the same.

For the 11 denominations, per member giving in 1992 inflation-adjusted dollars generally increased from 1921 to 1927, and then began to decline. This decline continued through the early years of the Great Depression. Giving increased slowly through 1943, the middle of World War II, and then began to grow more rapidly. Overall, the per member contribution for these 11 denominations increased in 1992 inflation-adjusted dollars from $130 in 1921 to $449 in 1995.

Using U.S. per capita disposable (after-tax) personal income accounts for the fact that the level of taxes changed throughout the century. As measured in 1992 inflation-adjusted dollars, U.S. per capita income was $4,479 in 1921, and $18,790 in 1995.

Giving as a Percentage of Income. For the 11 denominations, giving as a portion of income was above 3 percent from 1922 through 1933, the depth of the Great Depression. It began to fall in 1934 and, during the years of World War II, was around or below 2 percent. Giving as a percentage of income recovered after the war and was again at or above 3 percent from 1957 through 1963. A decline that began in 1961 continued through 1973 and leveled off at around 2.4 percent. Figure 2.1 presents these data.

As can be seen in Figure 2.2, an overall decline in giving as a percentage of income was also evident in the 29 denominations between 1968 and 1995. As measured in 1992 inflation-adjusted dollars, per capita disposable personal income increased by 68 percent between 1968 and 1995, from $11,211 to $18,790. With per member giving increasing only 33 percent,

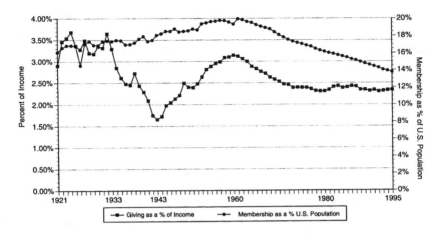

Figure 2.1. Giving as a Percentage of Income and Membership as a Percentage of U.S. Population, 11 Denominations, 1921-1995

SOURCE: empty tomb, inc. analysis, *Yearbook of American and Canadian Churches,* adjusted series; U.S. Bureau of Economic Analysis.
NOTE: Denominations (and their predecessors) included in the data set: American Baptist Churches in the U.S.A.; Christian Church (Disciples of Christ); Church of the Brethren; The Episcopal Church; Evangelical Lutheran Church in America; Moravian Church in America, Northern Province; Presbyterian Church (U.S.A.); Reformed Church in America; Southern Baptist Convention; United Church of Christ; The United Methodist Church.

from $349 to $463, the portion of income that per member contributions represented shrank, from 3.11 percent in 1968 to 2.46 percent in 1995.

Giving in the Roman Catholic Church. Although financial data have not been reported for the Roman Catholic Church since the early 1930s, survey data are available. An analysis of the work of Andrew Greeley and others suggests that giving as a percentage of income also decreased for Catholics between the 1960s and the mid-1980s (Ronsvalle and Ronsvalle 1988). A sampling of parishes found that household giving declined from 1991 to 1993 among Catholics in constant 1993 dollars (Harris 1994). In regard to trends, available Catholic data are consistent with the finding that there has been an overall decrease in per member contributions as a portion of income to the church during recent decades.[1]

---

1   The available data suggest that Catholic per member giving has been lower than Protestant giving. One analysis suggests that three cost-related variables—clergy compensation, clergy-to-parishioner ratio, and number of services per building—account in great measure for the difference (Ronsvalle and Ronsvalle 1995).

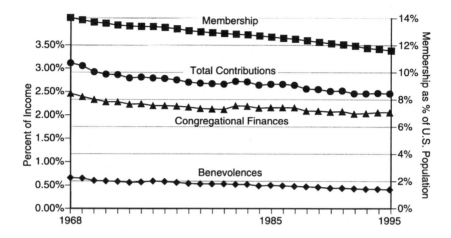

Figure 2.2. Giving as a Percentage of Income and Membership as a Percentage of U.S. Population, 29 Denominations, 1968-1995.

SOURCES: *Yearbook of American and Canadian Churches,* adjusted series; U.S. Bureau of Economic Analysis.

NOTE: Denominations included in the data set: American Baptist Churches in the U.S.A.; Associate Reformed Presbyterian Church (General Synod); Brethren in Christ Church; Christian Church (Disciples of Christ); Church of God (Anderson, IN); Church of God General Conference (Oregon, IL); Church of the Brethren; Church of the Nazarene; Conservative Congregational Christian Conference; Cumberland Presbyterian Church; Evangelical Congregational Church; Evangelical Covenant Church; Evangelical Lutheran Church in America; Evangelical Lutheran Synod; Evangelical Mennonite Church; Fellowship of Evangelical Bible Churches; Free Methodist Church of North America; Friends United Meeting ($ only; through 1990); General Association of General Baptists; Lutheran Church-Missouri Synod; Mennonite Church; Moravian Church in America, Northern Province; North American Baptist Conference; The Orthodox Presbyterian Church; Presbyterian Church (U.S.A.); Reformed Church in America; Seventh-day Adventists; Southern Baptist Convention; United Church of Christ; Wisconsin Evangelical Lutheran Synod.

Comparing NCC-Affiliated With NAE-Affiliated Denominations. Are the trends in giving identified above limited to denominations with a particular theological perspective? Eight communions in the data set of 29 denominations were affiliated with the National Association of Evangelicals (NAE) and eight denominations were affiliated with the National Council of Churches (NCC). When financial data from 1968, 1985, and 1995 for these 16 denominations were compared, two patterns became evident. First, in all three years per member giving in the NAE denominations was higher than per member giving in the NCC denominations. Second, this gap narrowed between 1968 and 1995. The NCC-affiliated denominations' per member contribution in 1992 inflation-adjusted dollars increased 46 percent, from $372 in 1968 to $545 in 1995. Meanwhile, the NAE-affiliated denominations' per member contribution increased 11 percent, from $688 in 1968 to $767 in 1995.

Analysis of the data for the NCC-affiliated denominations indicates that all of the increase was directed to congregational finances, while the per member contribution to benevolences in these congregations decreased from 1968 through 1995. During this period, these denominations also posted a decrease in total membership. Therefore, one might conjecture that the increase in giving was directed to congregational expenses in order to maintain a certain level of operations while receiving support from a smaller number of people.

In contrast, the real-dollar per member contribution in the NAE-affiliated denominations increased to both congregational finances and benevolences. These denominations posted a membership gain during the 1968-to-1995 period. However, it should be noted that the decline in giving as a percentage of income was sharper in the NAE-affiliated denominations than in the NCC-affiliated denominations. Giving as a percentage of income declined in the former from 6.1 percent in 1968 to 4.1 percent in 1995 (a 33 percent decline); it declined in the latter from 3.3 percent to 2.9 percent (a 13 percent decline) during those same years.

Overall, then, it appears that the generally held opinion that evangelicals are "better givers" than mainline members is correct in that per member giving was higher in the NAE-affiliated denominations both in terms of giving as a percentage of income and in terms of absolute dollars. However, given that the rate of decline in giving as a percentage of income was sharper for the NAE-affiliated denominations, it would also appear that the giving gap between the NAE- and the NCC-affiliated denominations has been narrowing.

Benevolences as a Proportion of Total Giving. A question in the financing of American religion is the extent to which congregations spend their money on their local operating expenses versus the extent to which they support the work of other religious activities, both denominational and nondenominational. One approach to this complex topic is to observe the percentage of congregational income that is devoted to benevolences. The Total Contributions data for the 29 denominations were reported in the two subcategories of Congregational Finances (internal operating expenses) and Benevolences ("the larger mission of the church"). A review of the data shows the number of real dollars going for benevolences remained essentially constant between 1968 and 1995 on a per member basis. It was $74 in 1968 and $77 dollars in 1995. Thus, 97 percent of the increase in per capita giving in inflation-adjusted dollars between 1968 and 1995 represents increased support of congregations' local operating costs. In 1968, 21 percent of congregational budgets were allocated for benevolences in these 29 denominations, dropping to under 17 percent in 1995. Figure 2.2 indicates that both congregational finances and benevolences were decreasing as a portion of income.

Benevolences Giving in The United Methodist Church. The United Methodist Church was formed in 1968 by the merging of two denominations. Over the years, its category of benevolences included pastor pension and health insurance, two expenditures that most other denominations include in congregational finances. Therefore, data for The United Methodist Church have not been strictly comparable with other communions. The United Methodist General Council on Finance and Administration provided data for the category of Connectional Clergy Support, which includes these pastor-related categories. The data indicate that United Methodist per member giving as a portion of income to Total Contributions was 2.27 percent in 1969 and 2.07 percent in 1995. When the amounts for Connectional Clergy Support were removed from the Benevolences subcategory, giving was 0.40 percent to benevolences in 1969 and 0.26 percent in 1995. This decline of 35 percent is similar to the decline of 37 percent observed in benevolences as a portion of income in the 29 denominations, which declined from 0.65 percent in 1969 to 0.41 percent in 1995.

FACTORS AFFECTING CHURCH SUPPORT

An analysis of the data presented above does not yield clear relationships among the three factors embodied in giving as a percentage of income, namely, giving, income, and membership. For example, between 1929 and 1933, income was declining, and yet giving as a percentage of income stayed above 3 percent, reaching a high point of 3.65 percent in 1932. During the 1950s, both income and giving as a percentage of income increased. Beginning in the 1960s, although income continued to increase, giving as a percentage of income began to decline.

This decline was accompanied by a change in membership patterns, as shown in Figure 2.1. Membership as a percentage of U.S. population was increasing in a fairly consistent fashion from 1921 until the 1960s. Post-1960s membership decline was not limited to these 11 denominations. As shown in Figure 2.2, membership as a percentage of U.S. population in the 29-denomination data set was also declining during the 1968-1995 period.

Research to date has not identified factors that have provided church leaders with effective tools to reverse the negative trends. Therefore, it is reasonable to suggest that a broad array of approaches be considered. Although the following example is limited in scope, it serves an exploratory function and may be illustrative of one type of research that may prove useful in the future.

A preliminary analysis of the relationship between giving to denominational overseas missions and membership change was conducted for five denominations. The percentage change from 1972 to 1991 for these two variables was compared. Two denominations—the Assemblies of God and the Southern Baptist Convention—saw an increase in per member giving to overseas missions and also experienced membership growth. Three denominations—the Evangelical Lutheran Church in America, the Presbyterian Church (U.S.A.), and The United Methodist Church—had a decline in overseas mission giving and also experienced membership decline during the same period. Given the small number of denominations in this initial analysis, this pattern should not be taken as firmly established. Even so, this correlation points to the need for further examination of the relationship between current members' willingness to support a cause beyond local congregational expenses and increase in membership (Ronsvalle and Ronsvalle 1995).

PRACTICAL CONCLUSIONS

The following basic trends have been described in this chapter. While per member inflation-adjusted dollars given were increasing, per member giving as a portion of income decreased since the 1960s, accompanied by a decline in membership as a percentage of U.S. population. The increases in per member dollars given were generally directed to internal congregational expenses rather than to benevolences. Three practical conclusions emerge from this overview.

1. The prolonged decline in giving as a portion of income suggests that technique-based attempts to increase church contributions have not had a major impact. As Americans' incomes have increased, giving statistics indicate that church members have not been convinced that they should continue

to give the same, or even an increased, portion of those incomes to their congregations. A tack different from stylistic solutions should be sought.

2. The portion of income directed beyond the local congregation to benevolences has declined more than total giving. Increases in inflation-adjusted per member giving have generally been directed to internal congregational expenses rather than to benevolences. Religious leaders should be attuned to this reallocation of resources at the congregational level. They should work on developing a vision that is attractive enough, and comprehensive enough, to convince church members to invest more of their resources in the agencies that the local congregation supports.

This idea is supported by another finding from a survey in a multiyear congregational study. Of those responding, 81 percent of the pastors and 94 percent of the regional officials agreed that "congregations do not have a clear overarching vision with which to challenge their members to improve their stewardship" (Ronsvalle and Ronsvalle 1996:53). It appears that, as concluded by the national advisory committee of the multiyear congregational study, "the church needs a positive agenda for the great affluence in our society" (Ronsvalle and Ronsvalle 1996:293). Such an intrinsic factor as "vision" may be an important element in both understanding, and perhaps reversing, negative giving trends.

3. Church members across the theological spectrum, both Protestant and Catholic, both evangelical and mainline, have been donating a smaller portion of their incomes to their congregations over a period of decades. Why people should give to the church needs to be reinterpreted and then effectively communicated to those who seek transcendence in their immediate circumstances. Church leaders may have to lay a renewed foundation, addressing basic attitudes toward money, the role of faith in relationship to giving, and why members should invest in the work of the church rather than spend their money in other ways. Such guidance will need to be grounded in a purpose that is more visionary than institutional maintenance of the local congregation or affiliated agencies, if the hope is that members will choose to increase their commitment to their churches.

REFERENCES

Harris, Joseph Claude. 1994. Personal correspondence, dated December 19, 1994, including spreadsheet titled "RUNSUMXLS: Preliminary Data Summary-1994, Catholic Contribution Study."

Hodgkinson, Virginia A., and Murray S. Weitzman. 1992. *From Belief to Commitment: The Community Service Activities and Finances of Religious Congregations in the United States, 1993 Edition.* Washington, DC: Independent Sector.

Ronsvalle, John, and Sylvia Ronsvalle. 1988. *A Comparison of the Growth in Church Contributions with United States Per Capita Income.* Champaign, IL: empty tomb, inc.

———. 1995. *The State of Church Giving Through 1993.* Champaign, IL: empty tomb, inc.

———. 1996. *Behind the Stained Glass Windows: Money Dynamics in the Church.* Grand Rapids, MI: Baker Books.

———. 1997. *The State of Church Giving Through 1995.* Champaign, IL: empty tomb, inc.

Chapter 3

Financing Historic
Black Churches

Calvin O. Pressley
Walter V. Collier

African Americans have supported their own religious institutions since the founding of Black congregations in the South during the 1770s. The subject of giving to the Black Church, however, has been obscured in the general literature on American religion, and it has only briefly been addressed by scholars of Black churches. Donations always have been of concern to churches, whatever their racial composition. Recently, however, increased pressure on Black churches to help with their community's social, health, and economic problems put the spotlight on the resources available to Black churches and on patterns of giving to these churches.

In 1997, the Institute of Church Administration and Management (ICAM), part of the Interdenominational Theological Center in Atlanta, conducted a two-level survey of Black congregations and their members. Modeled in part on the five-denomination survey described in Chapter 1 of this volume, this survey was designed to investigate the factors influencing giving to Black churches. We gathered congregational data from 141 churches in 13 locations and individual data from 3,637 members of those churches.[1]

---

1   Our 13 study sites were Houston, TX; Indianapolis, IN; Westchester County, NY; Memphis, TN; Monroe, LA; Atlanta, GA; Milwaukee, WI; Seattle, WA; Prince George's

This project represents the first time research of this scope has been undertaken in Black houses of worship, and we developed an innovative study design to secure the necessary data. Neither our selection of congregations nor our selection of individuals within those congregations was random. Given widespread suspicion among African Americans about the uses of social research, and because Black churches are not accustomed to revealing information to outsiders about their activities and finances, we believed it was necessary to build relationships with pastors and congregation members to earn their trust and gain their cooperation with this project. Because the field protocol we developed to achieve this goal was innovative and, we believe, successful, a description of it is in order.

The relationship building between the research project, on the one hand, and the congregations and their members, on the other, occurred on several levels. First, ICAM, as a respected organization within the Black Church community, provided the credibility needed to stimulate interest among the various Black denominations and congregations. Second, we selected a "Lead Consultant" in each of the 13 sites to act as liaison between ICAM and the local Black Church community and to identify and recruit local churches to participate in the study. Each Lead Consultant resided in the study site, had extensive pastoral experience and interdenominational ties, was knowledgeable about the local Black churches, and had an interest in stewardship within Black churches.

Third, each Lead Consultant recruited at least 10 churches from his or her area to participate in the study. Fourth, after congregations were recruited, ICAM's research team made a weekend visit to each site. The visit included a Friday evening clergy dinner, a Saturday morning Stewardship Breakfast at which members completed an anonymous questionnaire, and canvassing at the churches to survey members who did not attend the Breakfast. This canvassing occurred on both Saturday afternoon and Sunday, and involved distributing the questionnaires to church members at meetings of Bible study classes, men's groups, and other congregational affinity groups. Finally, pastors of the recruited congregations completed a church profile.

Although our sample of congregations matched fairly closely the denominational distributions of all congregations in each site, there were some biases that must be acknowledged. First, our sample was more urban than would be a random sample of all Black churches in the United States. Second, our sample probably overrepresented highly educated and highly active church members.

County, MD; Denver, CO; Brooklyn, NY; Los Angeles, CA; and Columbia, SC.

TABLE 3.1   Characteristics of Churches in ICAM Versus Lincoln and Mamiya
           Samples

	ICAM Sample	Lincoln and Mamiya Sample
Percentage Baptist	40	48
Percentage Methodist	38	34
Percentage Pentecostal	13	15
Percentage other denominations	9	3
Median number of members	450	198
Median annual revenue	$200,000	$27,412

NOTE: The Lincoln and Mamiya data ($n = 2,150$) are from Lincoln and Mamiya (1990:406).

Comparing the demographics of our sample with that of the general population of African Americans in the 13 study sites, we found some apparent biases in age, income, and education, with our sample having older, more educated, and higher-income persons.[2] However, this comparison may overstate the bias in our sample, given that the relevant comparison population is, after all, not the entire African American population in the study areas, but rather the church-going population. Unfortunately, data on the overall churchgoing population were not available for these communities.

Table 3.1 compares our congregations with Lincoln and Mamiya's (1990) early 1980s sample of congregations. Although our denominational distribution is very similar to theirs, the size difference is substantial. Our median congregation had 450 members, theirs had 198; our median congregation had annual income of $200,000, theirs had $27,412. Adjusting for inflation, the median Lincoln and Mamiya congregation received $42,900 annually in 1996 dollars. Given the almost 20-year gap between the studies, it may be that some of this difference represents a real increase in size and income of Black churches. It is impossible to tell, however, how much of this difference is produced by real change over time and how much represents bias in our sample toward larger and more affluent congregations. Given our design, it seems likely that a substantial proportion of this difference may have been produced by overrepresentation of larger congregations in our sample.

---

2   Our sample is 66 percent female, compared to 54 percent for the larger African American population in these sites; 64 percent in our sample are at least 44 years old, while only 35 percent of the over-18 populations in these sites are that old; 38 percent of our sample has at least a bachelor's degree, compared with 9 percent of the larger communities; and 39 percent of our sample lives in households with annual income of at least $51,000, compared with 23 percent of the larger community.

We conclude that our data are best understood as coming from a sample of larger, urban Black congregations and, within those congregations, they are best understood as coming from a sample of the highly educated, high-income, highly active members. Our results, then, should be taken as suggestive of patterns among this very important subset of the Black Church community.

The rest of this chapter presents an overview of some key results about church finances. Readers interested in more detail concerning either our methods or our findings should consult our final report (Collier & Associates 1998), from which this chapter is adapted.

FINDINGS

Table 3.2 presents basic results from the congregational profiles completed by clergy. This table shows the sources of the congregations' revenue, and it shows a breakdown of the congregations' spending. Median income for Black churches was $200,000, and median expenses were $181,500. As with predominantly white congregations, the vast majority of income comes from individuals' donations, and the vast majority of spending is on a congregation's local operations. Endowments are rare; capital campaigns are fairly common; and formal programs to encourage member giving—programs such as canvassing and pledging—are much less common than are sermons or testimonies on stewardship.

Turning to results from the sample of individuals, there were substantial differences among denominations in average levels of household income, church attendance, and giving. Significantly higher proportions of individuals had household incomes above $40,000 in Presbyterian, African Methodist Episcopal, and Baptist congregations than in the African Methodist Episcopal Zion, Pentecostal, Christian Methodist Episcopal, or Church of God in Christ (COGIC) congregations. At the same time, individuals in COGIC and Pentecostal churches attended services more frequently than individuals in other denominations. Individuals from these two denominations had the highest percentage of members who gave above the overall median annual household contribution of $1,930.

The obtained correlates of religious giving among African Americans were very similar to correlates of religious giving among white Americans (see Chapter 1 of this volume). When other characteristics were statistically controlled, the variables that significantly and positively affect individual giving by African American church members include income, age, level of par-

TABLE 3.2 Financial Characteristics of Black Churches in the ICAM Sample

Annual Income From:	Median Amount
Offerings, tithes, pledges	$127,000
Special fund-raisers	$5,485
Wills, bequests, gifts	$2,103
Investments	$5,500
Rents, fees	$5,150
Weddings, funerals	$850
Economic community projects	$19,972
Other (including capital campaigns)	$21,624
Total median income	$200,000

Annual Spending On:	
Church staff and operations	$90,000
Program subsidies	$7,628
Local mission work	$1,702
Global mission work	$1,179
Other expenses	$24,500
Total median expenses	$181,500

Other Financial Characteristics:	Percentage
Churches with ongoing campaigns for building construction or repair	51
Churches using pledge system	54
Churches with an endowment	13

Strategies to Encourage Giving:	Percentage Using
Sermons on stewardship	96
Appeals or testimonies	96
Distribution of written materials	87
Canvass some members in person	62
Canvass some members by phone	47
Canvass every member in person	40
Canvass every person by phone	34

NOTE: Median dollar amounts are calculated separately within each category of income and spending. Hence, the median amounts within the various income categories do not sum to $200,000, and the median amounts within the various spending categories do not sum to $181,500.

ticipation in the church, religiosity, spirituality, use of pledge cards, and believing that the church manages its money well.

While religiosity also proved to be a significant factor in giving within the Hoge et al. study on white congregations (described in Chapter 1), this particular factor was defined and measured in our study in a manner not directly comparable to how it was treated in that study. In our investigation, religiosity was defined in terms of frequency of involvement in religion outside of the church. Religiosity in the Hoge et al. study was defined as a person's approach to life being based on religion. We also looked at spirituality or a person's belief that he or she is connected to God or something larger than life. The spirituality factor was not included in the Hoge et al. study.

Interestingly, and consistent with patterns among whites, denominational differences in individual giving among African Americans remain even after relevant individual characteristics were controlled. That is, individuals in Pentecostal churches—either COGIC or other Pentecostal congregations—give at higher levels than people in other denominations, and this difference remains even after such things as income and level of participation in church were controlled.

Our survey also investigated the motivations for involvement in and giving to congregations. Respondents were asked what they looked for in the church experience. They were given a list of seven items and asked to rank them according to their importance. The seven items were spiritual support for everyday; spiritual support during a life crisis; fellowship; opportunities for worship services; music worship; social activism/community involvement; and religious education. Respondents were allowed to use the same rank more than once. "Spiritual support for everyday" emerged as the most important thing people sought in their church experience (average rank = 1). Fellowship, opportunities for worship services, religious education, and spiritual support during a life crisis had an average rank of 2. Less important to these respondents (average rank = 3) were music worship and social activism.

Consistent with this pattern are the results we obtained when asking respondents to rank, in order of importance, seven different reasons for giving to the church. The highest ranked reason was "to keep my covenant with God." The other reasons, in order of their average rank, were giving is a way of paying back blessings received; feeling that the church has a genuine need for donations; thinking that the programs sponsored by the church are appropriate; believing that the programs are helpful to the community; coming from a family that always gave to others in need; and feeling that giving leads to rewards in life. Together, these two ranking exercises lead us to conclude that, although social action and community service are important considerations for African Americans' church giving, they are less important than spiritual and religious considerations.

PRACTICAL CONCLUSIONS

Five practical conclusions emerge from this research:

1. It is important to note that, overall, the determinants of giving to churches seem basically similar for both African Americans and white Americans (compare Chapter 1 of this volume). The same basic factors—income, church attendance, religiosity—correlate with giving levels among individuals in both populations. Moreover, we observe denominational differences in giving that are similar to those observed among predominantly white denominations. Pentecostal denominations, in particular, seem to evoke higher levels of giving among both African Americans and whites. Practically, observing such similar patterns among both African Americans and whites suggests that strategies for fund-raising that work well for Black congregations may also work well for white congregations, and vice versa.

2. One strategy that seems to work similarly well in both Black and white congregations is worth emphasizing: pledge cards. Churches employing pledge cards as a means of committing members to give tended to receive more in donations than those that did not use pledge cards. Our results suggest that Black churches might benefit from increased use of pledge cards and, perhaps, other formal stewardship programs.

3. Our results suggest that member satisfaction with how the church manages its money significantly and positively influences levels of giving. Efforts by clergy to increase their members' satisfaction—via improved accounting procedures and enhanced communication with members about financial matters—might bear fruit.

4. The main motivations for giving to churches appear to be religious. This suggests that churches are more likely to increase donations by better meeting their members' religious needs than by increasing their social and political activism.

5. A final practical conclusion emerges more from our data collection process than from our results. We found that many churches did not have adequate records on their members' demographic characteristics. We believe that such information is vital for planning and targeting fund-raising efforts. Knowing members' income levels helps in setting realistic fund-raising goals; knowing members' occupations enables a pastor to identify individuals with skills that may be needed for particular ministries or programs. Congregations would benefit in several ways by gathering and maintaining better information about their people.

REFERENCES

Collier, Walter V., & Associates. 1998. *A Study on Financing Historic Black Churches. National Survey on Church Giving: A Research Report*. Atlanta, GA: Institute of Church Administration and Management.

Lincoln, C. Eric, and Laurence H. Mamiya. 1990. *The Black Church in the African American Experience*. Durham, NC: Duke University Press.

Chapter 4

Skewness Explained

LAURENCE R. IANNACCONE

Of all the behaviors that sustain religious organizations, none is more critical than individuals giving money. Without adequate income, congregations fold, denominations falter, and the faithful migrate to greener pastures. This chapter addresses a basic feature of giving to all voluntary associations, including religious organizations: skewness. Professional fundraisers consider skewness "a bedrock rule of thumb" relevant to virtually every setting, large or small, religious and nonreligious (Hoge 1994:103). In practice, it means that 20 percent of a congregation's members provide more than 80 percent of the giving. Inevitably, these people also exercise substantial power, for who can afford to alienate the few families that keep the church afloat? Yet the cause of skewness remains unclear. The "phenomenon begs for theoretical explanation" (Hoge 1994:103).

The explanation for skewness turns out to be surprisingly simple. As I will demonstrate in this chapter, the mathematics of giving makes skewness virtually inevitable. When varying rates of giving combine with varying incomes, a highly skewed distribution of dollar contributions *must* emerge. In practice, therefore, three facts suffice to generate skewness: (1) percentage rates of giving vary greatly from one person to the next; (2) income levels also vary greatly; and (3) income levels and giving rates are *not* strongly correlated.

AUTHOR'S NOTE: This chapter is adapted from "Skewness Explained: A Rational Choice Model of Religious Giving," by Laurence R. Iannaccone, *Journal for the Scientific Study of Religion* 36:141-57, 1997; used with permission.

Before turning to the analysis, it helps simply to look at data on religious giving. Figure 4.1 graphs the histogram of annual church contributions reported by a sample of about 2,300 adult Americans, respondents to the 1987-1989 General Social Surveys (Davis and Smith 1994). The horizontal axis shows the number of dollars contributed by each respondent, and the vertical axis shows the number of respondents contributing at each dollar level. The resulting distribution is heavily skewed: Whereas the majority of respondents contribute only a few hundred dollars or less, a small fraction of the population make contributions of several thousand dollars or more. This pattern is not unique to American Christianity. According to Fruehauf (1991:176, table 11-2) the largest 1.6 percent of all gifts to the 1987 Jewish Federation Campaigns (contributed by 13,000 donors who each gave $10,000 or more) accounted for nearly 60 percent of all the money collected. In contrast, the 450,000 donors who gave $100 or less accounted for 50 percent of all the givers but just 2 percent of the campaign total.

The practical importance of this pattern for religious organizations cannot be overemphasized—the relatively small number of large contributors literally keeps churches alive through donations that account for 80 percent to 90 percent of the funds used to pay pastors, operate church facilities, finance missions, and keep denominations afloat. This seemingly mundane fact goes a long way toward explaining the persistent (and inevitable) power of elites within *all* congregations and denominations, even those that embrace democratic values and nonhierarchical structures.

How are we to account for this pattern? It is evident in virtually all voluntary religious organizations regardless of their size, theology, or demographic composition. As Hoge (1993:3) observes, it is hard to believe that the underlying religious needs of individual members vary as widely as their contributions. Nor can we explain the observed pattern in terms of the underlying skewness of individual incomes. If typical churchgoers contribute a fixed percentage of their income, then contribution skewness would exactly mirror that of the underlying income distribution. The facts prove otherwise. Percentage rates of giving vary dramatically from one family to the next, and the skewness of contributions greatly exceeds that of income. The following simulations show that heavily skewed contributions will persist even when the underlying income distribution is *not* skewed.

As I already have noted, skewness can be explained in terms of three observable facts. First, percentage rates of giving vary dramatically from household to household. Second, incomes also vary. Third, there is little correlation between the *amount* of income a household has and the *share* of

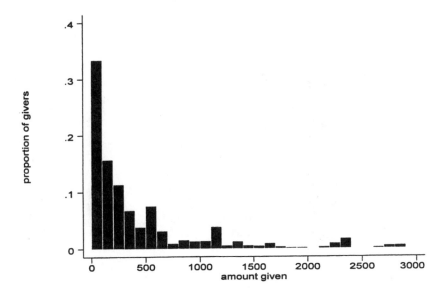

Figure 4.1. General Social Survey Contributions Data

income that it donates to religion. The following simulation shows how the explanation works.

Contribution Rates. All studies of giving find that the share of income given to religion varies greatly from one person to the next, depending mainly on a person's religiosity. The tendency to choose a share (rather than an absolute dollar amount) to give also is widespread. Many churches emphasize the notion of tithing rather than giving absolute amounts, and in practice one observes fairly similar *average* rates of giving—expressed as a percentage of income—across different income levels.

The share of income given to religion varies dramatically from one individual to the next, but surveys show that most people give between zero and 4 percent and the mean share is about 2 percent of income. My simulations therefore include a Share variable that is uniformly distributed between zero and 4 percent. By randomly generating 1,000 cases, I obtained the histogram in Figure 4.2.

Income. Although actual incomes are both widely dispersed and highly skewed in every city, state, and country, my simulation employs a distribution

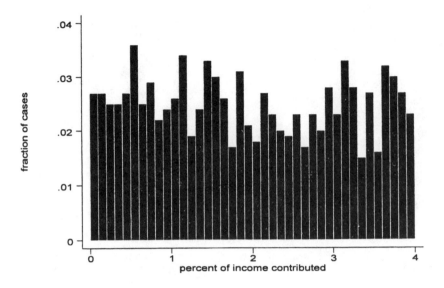

Figure 4.2. Simulated Contribution Shares (uniformly distributed)

that is nearly symmetric. I do so to prove that a skewed distribution of contributions will arise even when the underlying incomes are *not* skewed.
(When incomes *are* skewed the result becomes stronger still, since the skew
in the underlying income distribution tends to reinforce the skew caused by
the interaction between varying levels of income and varying rates of giving.)
Since actual household income was around $30,000 in the late 1980s, I gen-
erated an Income variable from a normal distribution (truncated at zero),
with a mean of $30,000 and a standard deviation of $15,000. Figure 4.3
graphs the resulting simulated income distribution.

Correlations. Decades of survey research prove that the actual relationship between religiosity and income is weak. Richer folks may attend church
a bit more or pray a bit less, but on the whole the impact of income is not
particularly great. Hence, the simulation assumes that a person's income is
not correlated with the proportion of income that that person gives. In other
words, in my simulation, these two variables are *independently* distributed.
The actual correlation between income and giving among General Social
Survey respondents is around –0.1, meaning that income explains only 1
percent of the variation in contributions.

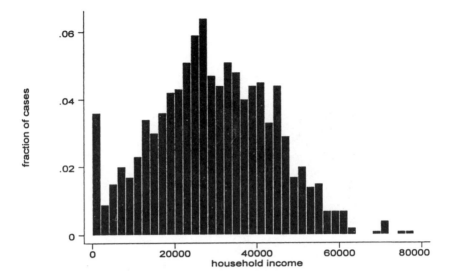

Figure 4.3. Simulated Incomes (truncated normal)

Taken together, this set-up allows me to simulate contributions as the product of Income and Share. People take their (randomly distributed) income, multiply by their (randomly distributed) propensity to give, and arrive at an actual dollar amount. In short, Contribution = Share × Income.

Figure 4.4 shows that the resulting distribution of contributions is heavily skewed. The skewness of contributions is especially striking given that both underlying distributions (Income and Share) are *not* skewed. Stated differently, the observed skewness is entirely the consequence of the *multiplicative* nature of the model. Almost *any* underlying distributions for Share and Income will produce the same sort of result. The simulated results in Figure 4.4 look strikingly similar to the actual distribution of giving observed in Figure 4.1—quite a few near zero, most folks in the few-hundred-dollar range, and a handful of much larger contributions.

A critic might dismiss these results as mere tautologies. After all, in simulations, what you get depends entirely upon what you assume. Yet this criticism misses several points. Skewness is indeed the inevitable consequence of facts (1), (2), and (3), but knowing this moves us past the mere observation that "contributions are skewed." With these facts in hand, we need no longer simply acknowledge the mystery of skewness; instead, we know its source.

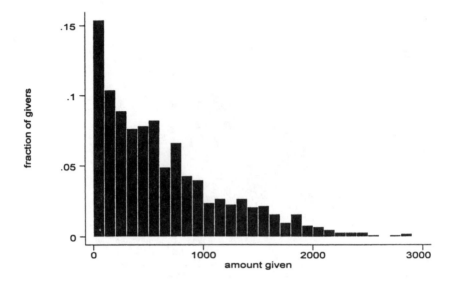

Figure 4.4. Simulated Contributions (simulated share × simulated income)

Moreover, as I illustrate in the article from which this chapter is adapted, facts (1), (2), and (3), the immediate source of skewness, are themselves rooted in still more basic features of economic life, religious commitment, and rational choice (Iannaccone 1997).

PRACTICAL CONCLUSIONS

Two critical practical insights emerge from this analysis.

1. Since skewness is built into the structure of religious giving, it must be viewed as a normal fact of life, not a symptom of organizational illness. A church leader can no more overcome the "problem" of skewness than a doctor can cure a healthy patient. Effective leaders must work *with* the fundamental features of the organization and its environment—railing against them can only lead to bitterness and disappointment.

2. This improved understanding of skewness leads to a second, more positive, insight. In tracing skewness back to incomes and rates of giving, this chapter directs our attention to the sources of giving. Rather than work (in-

effectively) to change the distribution of giving, religious leaders must take on a more daunting, but more fruitful, job: increasing the underlying level of commitment among members while perhaps also altering the congregational and denominational norms that shape perceptions concerning "normal" rates of giving. Neither of these are easy tasks, but they address the root causes of insufficient giving and expose the true nature of the problem that church leaders face. Besides, in the final analysis, even the hardest problem is easier to crack than an impossible one.

REFERENCES

Davis, James A., and Tom W. Smith. 1994. *General Social Surveys*. Chicago: National Opinion Research Center.

Fruehauf, Norbert. 1991. "The Bottom Line: Major Gifts to Federation Campaigns." Pp. 173-85 in *Contemporary Jewish Philanthropy in America*, edited by Barry A. Kosmin and Paul Ritterband. Savage, MD: Rowman and Littlefield.

Hoge, Dean R. 1993. "Theoretical Approaches for Explaining Levels of Financial Giving by Church Members." Paper presented at the Meetings of the Society for the Scientific Study of Religion, Raleigh, NC.

———. 1994. "Introduction: The Problem of Understanding Church Giving." *Review of Religious Research* 36:101-10.

Iannaccone, Laurence R. 1997. "Skewness Explained: A Rational Choice Model of Religious Giving." *Journal for the Scientific Study of Religion* 36:141-57.

Chapter 5

The Meaning of Religious Giving

SHARON L. MILLER

Denominations differ substantially in the average amounts that members give to congregations. This fact is well documented (see, e.g., Chapters 1 and 3 of this volume). However, the reasons for these differences are not clearly evident. Demographic differences among denominations have been largely discounted as significant sources of the variation in giving levels between denominations (Hoge and Yang 1994). Religious givers tend to look the same in all denominations. The highest givers tend to be between 40 and 60 years of age, married, with children. They are college graduates, earn above-average incomes, and are involved in their churches and communities. Orthodox beliefs and a strong personal faith are associated with higher giving, particularly among those who believe in a literal interpretation of the Bible. These individual differences influence giving levels *within* every denomination, but they do not explain differences *across* denominations. If demographic differences do not account for variations in levels of giving among denominations, then what does? Hoge and Augustyn (1997) acknowledge that there must be theological and institutional factors that explain some of the denominational differences in levels of giving, but these factors have yet to be fully explored and understood.

Drawing on my research in four congregations, representing four denominations, I argue that denominational culture is one of the unexplored yet important factors producing denominational differences in giving levels. Here, I will focus on only one aspect of a congregation's culture—individuals' understandings of *why* they give. There appears to be a substantial relationship between people's understanding of why they give and their self-reported giving levels. Those who talk about giving out of a sense of responsibility or obligation to their church and denomination give at a lower level than those who say that they give out of love for God, out of obedience to scripture, or to meet the needs of others. Furthermore, there are clear denominational patterns in how members responded to the question, "Why give?" These results suggest that denominational variations in cultures of giving, represented in part by how people articulate their reasons for giving, are connected to denominational differences in how much people ultimately give.

THE FOUR CHURCHES

I studied four churches, one each from these denominations: Presbyterian (U.S.A.), Assemblies of God, Roman Catholic, and Mennonite General Conference. The first three denominations were chosen because they had been included in previous research undertaken by Dean Hoge and his colleagues (see Chapter 1 of this volume). The giving levels in these three congregations correspond in rank order to the denominational differences reported in Chapter 1 of this volume. Individuals in the Assemblies of God congregation gave more than the Presbyterians, who gave more than the Catholics.

I also included a Mennonite church in my study because I hypothesized that that denomination's historical commitment to a critique of materialism, as well as its strong emphasis on missions and simple living, would influence its culture of giving. Wuthnow (1994) found that individuals' *perceptions* of their financial needs, over and above their "actual" needs, influence giving levels, and I suspected that I might be able to observe this by including a Mennonite congregation. Individuals in this congregation gave, on average, at levels very close to the average levels given by people in the Assemblies congregation. Qualitatively, these four churches can be grouped into two pairs in terms of average levels of individual giving. People in the Assemblies and Mennonite churches gave, on average, at levels similar to each other, and people in the Presbyterian and Catholic churches gave, on average, at levels similar to each other, but less than individuals in the other two churches.

The four congregations all are located in a midsized midwestern city and, according to regional denominational officials whom I contacted prior to this research, they are not atypical for their respective denominations. These congregations differed significantly from each other in size, average weekly attendance, and average age, but each was composed predominantly of middle-class whites.

I was a participant observer at each of these churches during the year it took to collect data for this study. I observed the rituals that surrounded the collection of money, interacted with parishioners in their own church settings, and listened to the implicit and explicit messages that were given regarding money. I collected denominational materials dealing with money, tithing, and stewardship, as well as sermons and articles on money or stewardship delivered or written by the clergy of these congregations. I also conducted extensive face-to-face interviews with clergy at each church. The heart of the data collection, however, was face-to-face interviewing with a randomly selected sample of regular participants—not necessarily formal members—in each congregation. The main goal of these interviews was to learn what meanings respondents attached to religious money and religious giving. In this chapter, I focus mainly on respondents' answers to the open-ended question, "Why do you give money to your church?" Readers should see my dissertation (Miller forthcoming) for more detail about my methods and for more thorough discussion of cultures of giving in these four congregations.

FINDINGS

Table 5.1 shows how often respondents in each congregation mentioned one of eight different types of reasons for giving to their churches. The relevant question was open-ended, and responses were tape-recorded and transcribed. This table therefore represents a content analysis of respondents' transcribed responses to the question, "Why do you give money to your church?" A respondent's answer could contain more than one type of response.

The results show that there are clear denominational differences in how people typically conceptualize their giving. As Table 5.1 shows, people in both the Catholic and the Presbyterian churches viewed their giving primarily as a responsibility or obligation to the organizational maintenance of the congregation. Virtually all the Catholic and Presbyterian respondents talked about their giving in this way, compared with only about half of the Assemblies and Mennonite respondents.[1] Presbyterians and Catholics also were far

1 All the percentage differences mentioned in this chapter are statistically significant at least at the .05 level.

TABLE 5.1 Stated Reasons for Giving to Church

	Catholic	Presbyterian	Assemblies	Mennonite
Percentage who say they give:				
To pay the church bills	53	44	0	5
Out of responsibility or obligation as a member of this church	93	89	44	60
Because I am giving to God or Because I love God	0	6	39	15
To obey the Bible or God	13	11	100	45
Out of thankfulness for all I have	27	6	11	50
To meet the needs of others or For missions	20	28	22	50
Because everything I have is God's	7	6	28	40
Because God will take care of my needs or Because God will bless me if I give	13	0	67	10

NOTE: These percentages are based on interviews with 15 Catholics, 18 Presbyterians, 18 Assemblies of God members, and 20 Mennonites.

(handwritten annotation in left margin: "Prosperity gospel")

more likely than members of the other two churches to refer to the fact that the church bills must be paid.

While also acknowledging an institutional responsibility to support the church, Mennonites and Assemblies of God respondents were more likely to emphasize other reasons for giving than were Presbyterians and Catholics. Mennonites spoke more often than others about giving out of a sense of thankfulness and giving to meet the needs of others. Assemblies respondents *all* said that they gave out of obedience to God or the Bible—a response that was given by about half the Mennonites and by virtually no Presbyterians or Catholics. Assemblies respondents also were much more likely than others to say that God would bless or reward them for giving. The following paragraphs elaborate these basic differences.

The patterns in Table 5.1 suggest that Presbyterians and Catholics give primarily out of a concern with institutional survival. Here is a typical response, from an older Presbyterian woman: "The church is a valuable institution . . . and we give to it because that is where we have our membership." In the words of a Catholic respondent, "It is a definite obligation to help support your church. If you belong to any organization you support them . . . You have a deep feeling of responsibility." Catholics also often connected their obligation to give to the fact that their children attend the church's parochial school. Both Presbyterian and Catholic respondents frequently mentioned the numerous bills the church must pay, including the pastor's salary. They seemed to view their own giving as another bill to pay.

Only two Catholic respondents and two Presbyterian respondents claimed to tithe (give 10 percent of their income) to the church. It is note-worthy that all four of these individuals connected their giving to reasons other than support for the institution, such as giving out of obedience or thankfulness. The remaining respondents either gave a lower proportion of their income, usually between 2 percent and 3 percent, or they gave an arbitrary weekly or monthly amount. The amounts they chose to give seem to be a combination of what they think is their "fair share" of the church budget and what they think their finances can bear. Often this assessment took place some time ago and has not been revisited recently. One well-to-do respondent reported, "We pledge $20 a week. I don't know how we came up with that; we have given that much for years and years."

Like Presbyterians and Catholics, Mennonite respondents commonly expressed a sense of responsibility or obligation to support their congregation as an organization. Other themes, however, also were mentioned. Half of the Mennonite respondents said that they give out of thankfulness for all they have, and half connected their giving to meeting the needs of others. Nine out of the 20 (45 percent) said that they give because the Bible or God commands it, and eight (40 percent) said that they give back to God because everything they have is God's. Typical is this response from a young couple: "We feel that we want to support our church. We like our church and we feel that it is the right thing to do. . . . We are giving to God. . . . We want the benefit to go to others as well as ourselves."

Giving as the responsibility of a church member was also a common theme among Assemblies respondents. However, like the Mennonites and unlike the Presbyterians and Catholics, other themes also were prevalent. Most strikingly, *all* respondents from the Assemblies of God church talked about their giving as an obedient response to God. On more than one occasion, Assemblies respondents brought their Bibles to the interview in order to point out the verses that commanded a tithe. Seven of 18 (39 percent) explicitly said that they viewed their offering as a gift to God, and the church is simply a channel for that gift. One interesting implication of viewing an offering in this manner is an apparent lack of concern with how the money is used after it leaves their hands. Typical is the response from this single woman: "My responsibility is to give my 10 percent tithe. . . . I am being obedient to what God would have me do. How the people use what I give they are responsible to the Lord for."

Two thirds of Assemblies respondents said that, if they give faithfully, God will take care of them. Although the pastor of the Assemblies church explicitly condemned a "Prosperity Gospel"—give and you will be blessed—a version of this message clearly came through in the songs, prayers, and messages I heard delivered from the pulpit during my visits to worship services at this congregation. Worshipers are repeatedly reminded during services that "God is in control, God will take care of all your needs, everything you have belongs to God." Participants in this congregation seem to have heard this message; all but one respondent claimed to give at least 10 percent of their income to the church.

This last point—the connection between the preaching people hear and the meanings they attach to religious giving—raises the important issue of the mechanisms that might be producing denominational differences in how people understand their giving. The Assemblies example in the previous paragraph suggests that the explicit teaching and preaching of the clergy are important. Also important, however, are the rituals, content, and practices of the worship services and other congregational events in which teachings about giving and money are embedded. Individuals from the Assemblies and Mennonite churches, as we have seen, both connect their giving to things other than the congregation's institutional needs. Might these individual-level meanings be connected to collective practices in these congregations?

The Assemblies of God church begins the main Sunday service with an hour of prayer and praise. During this portion of the service the presence of God is made manifest through music, prayer, prophecy, and speaking in tongues. At least temporarily, the chasm between humanity and divinity is narrowed through ritualized collective effervescence. The offering is collected in the midst of this hour. It seems plausible that presenting one's offerings in this sort of context would support the understanding that money is given directly to God. As one Assemblies respondent put it, "If I withhold giving I am withholding worship." The act of giving in this congregation is embedded in a total worship experience that makes it easy to see one's giving as a reflection of one's trust in God.

Particularly striking in the morning worship service at the Mennonite church is the congregation's manifest attention to the needs of the world. Each service has a lengthy period in which people share prayer requests and announcements. In addition to mentioning local individual needs, such as requesting prayer for someone who is ill, it also is common during this time to hear prayer requests for such things as peace in the Persian Gulf, missions in Haiti, or the work of a volunteer in Cambodia. Announcements remind people of tutoring opportunities at an African American church, volunteer night at the local homeless shelter, work on a Habitat for Humanity house, and so on. Sixteen of the 20 Mennonite respondents were involved in some form of volunteer work for the church or the community. It seems plausible, then, that these collective practices have something to do with the fact that Mennonite giving is more often connected to meeting the needs of others than it is in the other churches.

In addition, both the Mennonite and the Assemblies churches challenge the material emphasis in mainstream American culture. More than in Presbyterian or Catholic sermons that I read or heard, sermons in both the Mennonite and Assemblies churches urged people to differentiate clearly between their material needs and their material desires. Sermons in these churches also more commonly invite believers to trust in God for their present and future needs. The Assemblies of God church regularly holds adult education classes on managing personal finances, and the Mennonite church periodically holds a discussion group focused on lifestyle issues.

By contrast, both the Catholic church and the Presbyterian church seem to avoid explicit mention of finances and money, except for the annual pledge drive in the fall. The emphasis of the pledge drive is focused on meeting the budget of the church. Thus, it is not surprising that people view their giving as an obligation. They give willingly, often generously, to meet this budget, but members rarely talk about their giving in other than a purely pragmatic manner. Members often view their giving as paying the bills, and just as they are conscientious with their own home finances, they seek to be responsible and careful with the church's finances. To give 10 percent of their income to the church is seen by most as extravagant, excessive, and, indeed, unnecessary. The bills are, after all, being paid.

In response to the question, "Does giving do anything for you personally?" I was often met with blank stares from Presbyterian and Catholic respondents. A typical response was given by a Presbyterian man: "It doesn't elevate me to a higher plateau because I am giving; it is because I know this is what is necessary to maintain the building." A Catholic woman responded, "I get the sense that I am helping, but as far as making me go out and dance in the street, no." One consequence of this pragmatic approach to giving is that people appear to be much more critical of how money—*their* money—is being spent at the church. They are quick to judge expenditures as "wasteful" or "foolish."

PRACTICAL CONCLUSIONS

 In summary, I found denominational differences in the meanings individuals attach to giving. These differences in meaning seem to be connected to the amounts that people give. If people believe that the reason they should give is to maintain the services of the church, then they give enough to do that and little more. If giving is seen as part of a larger scheme—representative of one's relationship with God or meeting the needs of others—then more is given. These differences were connected to variations *within* congregations in how much people gave. That is, no matter the denomination, those who explicitly connected their giving either to their relationship with God or to meeting the needs of others gave more generously than those who spoke only of paying the bills. Unlike demographic correlates of giving within denominations, however, it seems that these differences in meaning might help to generate variations *across* denominations in the amounts that people give. Importantly, the differences in meaning described in this chapter seem to reflect broader differences among these congregations in how giving fits into the set of collective practices and rituals that together constitute a congregation's culture.

Three practical conclusions emerge from these results.

1. Denominational differences in giving levels reflect, in part, the larger complex of religious practices and traditions within which giving occurs. Different ritual and programmatic contexts seem to generate both different meanings attached to giving and different levels of giving. This institutional embeddedness of giving suggests that substantially altering church members' giving levels may require change that is deeper and wider than merely preaching more stewardship sermons or implementing a new pledge system.

2. These findings also suggest that individuals give more when their giving is connected to something other than the organizational maintenance of the church. Pastors and church leaders might see better results by focusing financial appeals more on the religious value of giving and on the mission of the church rather than on the organizational needs of the congregation.

3. These findings suggest that the rituals—prayers, songs, announcements, exhortations—surrounding the collection of the offering might influence how people understand their giving. If these rituals focus attention on the institutional life of the church, people are more likely to interpret their giving as supporting the institution. If the rituals focus attention on the needs of others or on a relationship with a transcendent being, then giving is placed in quite a different context.

REFERENCES

Hoge, Dean, and Boguslaw Augustyn. 1997. "Financial Contributions to Catholic Parishes: A Nationwide Study of Determinants." *Review of Religious Research* 39:46-60.

Hoge, Dean, and Fenggang Yang. 1994. "Determinants of Religious Giving in American Denominations: Data From Two Nationwide Surveys." *Review of Religious Research* 36:123-48.

Miller, Sharon. forthcoming. "The Cultural and Symbolic Meaning of Religious Money in America." Doctoral dissertation, Department of Sociology, University of Notre Dame.

Wuthnow, Robert. 1994. *God and Mammon in America.* New York: Free Press.

Chapter 6

Historical Myths
About Financing
American Christianity

JAMES HUDNUT-BEUMLER

When people cannot get facts, they will settle for myths. When people are faced with facts, they will often prefer the myths they are being asked to reject in favor of facts. In seeking to understand how American Christians have economically structured and financed their churches, it becomes quickly evident that myths play a large role in what passes for knowledge. As in any relatively new field of inquiry, reports of many early investigations in this field are filled with laments for the dearth of information about the way things were in the past.

As a historian interested in the topic of financing American religion, it has intrigued me that this absence of facts has not prevented conjecture, wishful thinking, and assumptions about the past from motivating some present-day inquiries. Thus, I enter the conversation of this volume with an eye to separating realities from myths. This chapter seeks to suggest some alternatives to the interpretations I have heard offered for the way things are in the economic conditions of contemporary American Christianity. Each of the explanations here labeled as a "myth" is something that I have heard passed off as a truism, either from a church pulpit or at a stewardship conference, or as a strong hypothesis at a gathering of scholars working on this material from a sociological or economic analysis framework.

The historian's job in this domain is to answer the perennial question, "How long has this been going on?" As we shall see when we examine the questions implicit in these myths, sometimes the answer will be, "They are not going on even now." Here, then, are seven statements that, judged against my in-progress examination of the historical record, appear to be myths.

MYTHS ABOUT CAPITAL

In ordering the fiscal houses of religious bodies, it is not unusual for acrimony to break out around issues of how many resources ought to be expended immediately and which resources should be used to acquire or improve the bodies' physical assets. That myths about capital should develop should not be surprising in churches with an abiding ambivalence about wealth and its possession. Still, it is striking how often the blame for current financing woes is laid at the feet of religious buildings.

> *Myth #1.* "Part of why we are experiencing a loss of financial wherewithal in mainstream Christianity is that congregations are spending outrageous sums on themselves in the form of new, enlarged, or renovated church buildings. For most of American religious history, once a congregation built its house of worship it kept using it without having to add family life centers and suchlike to keep up with the mega-churches."

The reality, of course, is more complex. Some observers of the contemporary scene have written as if the problem with current giving (and particularly with giving beyond the local congregation) is that church people have recently developed a taste for spending lavish amounts on plant and equipment. In fact, when we look at American Protestant, Catholic, and Jewish congregations over a period of 350 years, a pattern develops. Far from only caretaking what was built by generation one, each adult generation of a vital congregation appears to engage in a major building project. The New England church on the green that looks unchanged has probably gone through eight major renovations or restorations to attain that untouched quality it now exudes.

Something more significant than taste-oriented redecorating appears to be going on. I hold the view that what we are, in fact, witnessing is a marking out of sacred space by investing time and energy in those places and spaces that take on a spiritual significance. The proud claim, "We built this church," even if what was built is only a family life center, stands as a generation's witness to its faith in the institution of church, if not also its faith in God.

Since the implied criticism in the myth is that capital expenditures might have been more productively used in programmatic mission, one might well reverse the direction of the interpretive strategy and ask a new question. Are there multigenerational expressions of congregational life that feature lots of positively externalized mission, but that do not include improvements of the congregation's capital stocks from time to time?

Myth #2. "After World War II, suburbanization and the consumer society brought with it a disposable mentality about our church buildings, camps, and centers that has cost organized religion dearly in the subsequent years."

If the first myth implies that religious people loved their buildings too much, the second argues that they respected their old buildings too little. Again the myth envisions a fairly recent phenomenon. In fact, by examining local and diocesan church histories, one quickly discovers that congregations in the nineteenth century abandoned property for other locations far more frequently than in the mid- to late twentieth century. Indeed, most religious capital assets placed in service 80 years ago are still in service. Surely that claim could not be made for retail trade establishments, restaurants, or factories!

On the other hand, some things have changed in the twentieth century. From 1960 onward, the scope and scale of new religious buildings grew. At the same time, real land costs increased and average congregation size declined. The phenomenon is not dissimilar to that of smaller 1990s families living in more spacious, more luxurious homes than those that housed the larger families of the 1950s. In each case, the household unit (the congregation and the family, respectively) is trying to afford and occupy more space in accordance with changing tastes. The contemporary family solves its housing dilemma by putting an additional adult out to work, but the average contemporary congregation finds itself with fewer contributing adults. The emergence of this gap between the buildings congregations would like to have and their ability to pay for them is masked in part by deferred maintenance on older buildings and a differentially greater rise in the standard of living in exurban metro areas where most new churches are built.

MYTHS ABOUT LABOR

The largest recurring expense in most religious organizations is for personnel. It is true that Protestant ministers do not command the incomes of ordained personnel in the past. Popular interpreters tend to be divided, however, on whether to blame the influx of women into the profession or to attribute the pattern to a long and inexorable journey toward secularization.

> *Myth #3.* "The entrance of women into the ministry of Protestant churches has driven down real clergy incomes to the point where the ministry is in danger of becoming a 'pink-collar ghetto.' "

While women ministers have taken jobs that would have gone unfilled 40 years ago, the decline in real clergy income and in income relative to comparable professions such as the law, medicine, or teaching is a secular trend predating the entrance of women into the field in significant numbers. In our own studies of clergy household income we compared Methodist ministers' incomes against changes in wage and price levels over more than 120 years. What we discovered was that, from a high point in 1960, when ministers' mean income nearly equaled median family income in the United States, real clergy income spiraled downward after 1968 so that, by the late 1970s, clergy made less than half of what a typical middle-class family spent in a year. Moreover, although clergy incomes more than maintained purchasing power relative to inflation across a century, they did not grow anything like the economy as a whole. Thus, while the American standard of living soared and added a vast proportion of the population to the ranks of the middle class, by 1980 the average Methodist minister could not claim much more than a tenuous place in that middle class. Up and down the socioeconomic rankings of clergy by denomination, the same thing was happening. The ministry was slipping as a profession; and all these changes took place before a significant number of women were ordained.

> *Myth #4.* "The key moment in the long descent of the clergy from respected gentlemen to barely middle-class professionals was the nineteenth-century move from 'office' to 'profession.' Once the clergy abandoned their claim to exclusive rights of spiritual leadership, a free market of church and leader choices assured their devaluation as culturally honored authorities."

When it comes to how and in what ways ministers are valued, three twentieth-century moments are most important. The first was the time of the fundamentalist-modernist battles, battles that de-centered religious leaders from prominence among cultural elites. The minister in 1890 was a far more respected community figure than the minister of 1935. Internal theological disputes opened up the profession to scrutiny in indirect and unintended ways that did not help its status. The second was a similar impact wrought by Vatican II on the status of priests. Exposing the mysteries to secular light and vernacular dispute made the priesthood less "special." A third important moment occurred in the 1960s and 1970s and affected all religious leaders. I refer to the voluntary abdication of many clergy, for principled ideological and theological reasons, from their traditional position as arbiters of moral and theological truth. Rarely has a professional group conspired so completely in its own devaluation.

MYTHS ABOUT FINANCE

When contemporary interpreters of the financing situation are not worrying about where the money is going—be it to people or buildings—they are apt to be concerned with where it is coming from and why there does not seem to be as much available as in some time of happier memory. Indeed, the strongest myths in this entire area are those concerning how money "always" used to be raised and given. The common pattern is to juxtapose the faithfulness of the past to the feckless giving practices of the present.

Myth #5. "Back in the old days, everyone (at least in Protestant churches) tithed."

In fact, tithing began to be actively promoted in American Protestantism only in the nineteenth century, after the town finance, subscription book, and pew rent methods of raising church funds each failed to produce enough revenue. Preaching the tithe may have produced more income, but few major religious groups in American history have ever succeeded in getting its adherents, on average, to give anything close to one tenth of their incomes. Recent studies suggest that a range of 2.5 percent to 4 percent of income is a more typical giving range among Protestants, with a somewhat lower range for Catholics (see Chapter 1 in this volume).

Myth #6. "The designated giving movement represents a complete rejection of the theological principle of unified giving that underlies Christian stewardship."

Examining the history of fund-raising for religious causes, and particularly charitable causes, one finds that different ethics at different times present themselves as the "most Christian way to do things." Unified giving, the alternative to "designated giving," is simply the most recent successful claimant to the title of "most Christian way to do things." The most important insight to emerge from studying the ebb and flow of "Christian" ways to raise money is that unified approaches to religious finance are highly dependent upon social consensus. By contrast, periods of high levels of social change appear to lead to the formation of new causes, which must take their need for funds directly to potential givers, either as individuals or as churches. Such was the case in the antebellum and Social Gospel periods, times of various attempts to reform society. Similarly, social change is probably the dynamic behind the proliferation of new charities making direct appeals since 1980, appeals growing out of contemporary social problems such as homelessness, AIDS, international globalization, and increasing income disparity. Other periods—the 1910s and 1920s and between 1945 and 1960—are characterized by significant trust in large-scale institutions like denominations and charitable federations to carry on efficiently the agreed-upon social agenda emerging from the previous generation of religious-social movements. The theological overlay of the myth as stated above serves mostly to obscure the level of social disagreement among contemporary Christians.

A MYTH ABOUT
TECHNOLOGICAL INNOVATION

Over the past two centuries, American Christianity has served as an unusual crucible in which a tradition reaching back centuries has melded with rapid technological and social change and produced denominations, colleges, social movements, and an amazing degree of religious vitality. As much as Americans are proud of their receptivity to technological innovations, there are reasons to argue that technical advance has not always resulted in healthier, more faithful churches.

Myth #7. "Organized Catholicism and Protestantism adapted to technological innovation reasonably well until the mid-twentieth-century introduction of television."

It is a commonplace that television has uniquely challenged religion's hold on people's time and loyalties. Viewed historically, however, television appears less than unique. Instead, television should be viewed as another in a long series of technological and cultural advances that were perceived as threatening to churches' hold on the hearts of their people. Reading novels, dancing, playing cards, and going to the theater or to the movies were all opposed by religious groups as they became culturally available because they were perceived as either counter to the gospel or as simply more amusing than sitting at the mass or listening to a sermon.

PRACTICAL CONCLUSIONS

Looking carefully at the past can help us to see our own contemporary situation more clearly. Five specific practical conclusions emerge from this very brief overview of the historical record on the financing of American religion.

1. Tithing is not an eternal practice from which the current generation has fallen away. Appeals that present tithing as a common practice of the past are of dubious historical validity.

2. Comparing one's self or one's people to the past risks rendering the past better in memory than it was in fact. The most important thing contemporary Christian leaders can ask their followers is this: What are the resources *we have now* to do the things we believe are important? Holding up the example of ancestors has little historical justification.

3. Financial pressures related to physical plants are not new. They are a perennial part of American religion. Building and managing a physical plant of appropriate size has always been key to a congregation's financial health.

4. The historical record shows a seesawing between support for unified giving and support for designated giving. The popularity of one or the other at a given time is more likely to reflect contemporary social conditions than any clear and unambiguous theological principle.

5. Congregations should face the fact that salaries being paid to clergy have declined very substantially in real terms over the second half of the twentieth century. This trend may very well affect religious organizations' ability to attract the best and brightest to its leadership ranks.

Chapter 7

Why Give?

ROBERT WOOD LYNN

Why give? Any answer to this question involves an appeal to some authority, and Protestants have struggled since the early days of the American republic to locate the authority that would support the appeal of one church member asking another to give money to a Christian cause. This question becomes all the more difficult in a democracy where the spirit of religious individualism remains a potent force. In the United States, appeals to the official authority of the clergy have carried little weight when the conversation turns to money. Only a slim minority of denominations have been able to establish enforceable standards that regulate giving, while most Protestants have relied upon the persuasive powers of certain *teachings* about giving. However, what appeals to one generation can wear thin in the next one. So the search for authoritative arguments continues in every era.

Each generation's answer to the question—"Why give?"—reveals something about that era's understanding of the church and its mission to the world. This chapter traces the history of some of those changing understandings among mainstream Protestants, dividing the past 150 years into three periods. The "Republic of Benevolence" characterizes the antebellum years. Then comes the discovery and celebration of the "Good Steward" in the first quarter of this century. The final section deals with the gradual implosion of "stewardship" in the decades after World War II. This chapter provides an overview of changing teachings about giving, and a very partial overview at that. Readers interested in more nuance and detail should see the larger work (Lynn 1995) from which this chapter is adapted.

A REPUBLIC OF BENEVOLENCE:
1820S-1850S

The church and agency leaders of the antebellum era dreaded the "business of charitable solicitation," but it proved an inescapable necessity. The old colonial order was rapidly disappearing, and by 1820 only one state, Massachusetts, had even the remnants of an established church. Government subsidies for parishes belonged to a fading past and churches could not rely on the coercive force of the state to raise their much needed funds. The church was now dependent on volunteerism and the art of persuasion in order to provide support for ministers, religious institutions, and churches.

Some Protestant leaders, in their search for an authority that would give power and meaning to their requests for support, invoked a vision of the future. This vision provided the needed impetus to give generously, and it offered a way of understanding America's role in the present and future world. A sense of emergency often pervaded Protestant prose of this period. One finds allusions to enemies as well as to comrades in arms. The list of enemies included Roman Catholics (first and foremost), other religious opponents, and, of course, "infidels" of various persuasions. Political fears also were invoked—worries about America's decline, if not its disintegration; the power of its enemies abroad and at home; or even a fear about the demise of civilization itself. This should come as no surprise to anyone who has examined the tactics implicit in those fund-raising letters that arrive in our mail today. Fear often looms large in American appeals for money.

Although some people give out of fear, they also give to an embodied future. Some antebellum writers knew that hope for a desired, shared future also could stimulate giving. The most common and powerful expectation centered upon the destiny of America as a religious force in the world. Christendom's future depended upon what happened in this nation, they asserted. This hoped-for "victory" would require sacrificial giving from Christians in this country. The coming triumph is so close, they often asserted, that now—not tomorrow or next year—is the moment in which we were being called to give everything for the cause. These are not the usual times, and so they demand heroic givers. Out of this stream of thinking emerged a characteristic phrase that one still occasionally hears in high-pressured capital campaigns—the "sacrificial gift." There also was a discernible shift in this era from a focus on the philanthropy of the upper classes to an appeal to the ordinary American. In the benevolent republic, Christians would become good citizens by learning how to give in a responsible fashion.

Meanwhile, church leaders set out to establish major new institutions and urged members to embrace new—and often very expensive—causes. The romance of foreign missions sometimes obscured the hard reality of just how costly it was to send missionaries abroad. In addition, there was the home missions movement to support, Bibles and tracts to be distributed, Sunday schools to start, ministers to educate, and moral reforms to inaugurate across the immense spaces of a growing country. There was intense competition for money, coming from all these agencies and church bodies, and the roving financial "agent" (or fund-raiser) became a new fixture on the American scene. These roving agents from the various societies (such as the American Tract Society, the American Bible Society, the American Sunday School Union, and the American Home Mission Society) were dispatched across the country to organize local branch societies and to raise money for the home offices.

It was a lonely and formidable job. The pressure of time and the requirement of eliciting as many commitments and pledges as possible forced the agents to preach simple sermons with mass appeal. When there was any hint of apathy on the part of the audience, the agents were often tempted to resort to callous manipulation. The ensuing results were self-defeating, for they strengthened a growing perception of benevolent agents as hucksters. Their apparently incessant begging for money aroused resentment and resistance. By the mid-1830s the cries of protest against the "swarm" of agents became louder, and a few began to ask if the agent system was even necessary.

Up to the 1850s, most Protestant fund-raisers had focused attention upon some large, compelling cause beyond the individual giver—the foreign missions movement, for instance. Samuel Harris, a Massachusetts pastor, was convinced that people's lack of financial generosity was due to the sin of covetousness. He chose to turn his audience's gaze inward and there to confront the souls of American Protestants caught in the contradictions of greed. What was needed was obedience to a rigorous discipline. Harris found the solution in "systematic benevolence." Benevolence, by itself, could evaporate into sentiment. The transforming presence of a system could provide not only order but also endurance and staying power against the temptations of money.

The verse that became the bedrock of this theology of giving was I Corinthians 16:2. "Upon the first day of the week let every one of you lay by him in store, as God hath prospered him, that there be no gatherings when I come." This verse was literally a "God-send"! First, the idea of a "law" governing giving brought comfort to a population looking for moral order and security. Second, it opened the way for Harris and others to present the idea of proportionate giving: One should give according to one's means. The phrase, "as God hath prospered him," proved indispensable in this theology. Third, it encouraged the habit of contributing in a regular fashion, rather than succumbing to the vagaries of impulse after a particularly moving charity sermon. Harris recommended another regular exercise: Christians should keep records of their gifts as a way of struggling against the considerable powers of self-deception in matters of money.

If this "system" of giving were adapted by church members it would do away with the society agents. "Let this system be adopted," Samuel Harris wrote, "and the funds of the benevolent societies would flow in unsolicited gifts, and the expense of collecting agencies would cease" (Harris 1850:128). Here was a practical, realistic way of providing constantly growing support for the churches. Once this practice is implanted in the lives of American Protestants, it would free the church from the indignities of fund-raising.

Others went even farther. The blessings of "systematic giving" would bring order, serenity, and even prosperity into the lives of givers because of four factors: (1) The "system" in systematic benevolence would promote efficiency in the lives of givers, for they would have to keep accurate records of income and benevolent expenditures. (2) Such efficiency makes possible greater thrift. (3) Thrift begets prosperity and savings. (4) Prosperity makes it possible for the individual to be even more generous in giving. The call to systematic giving would be influential well into the twentieth century.

THE GOOD STEWARD: 1870S-1930S

Some voices continued to raise the question, "Why give?" One was Mary Dodge, a journalist active in the 1870s. Dodge's chief complaint centered on the question of authority, for she believed that there was no possible justification for one Christian to tell another how much to give. "You have no more right to dictate a man's charities," she noted, "than you have to dictate his courtship" (Hamilton 1877:137).[1] Just as courtship or romantic love had become a profoundly personal or private concern, so any decision about giving money was now made in the private domain. No one may infringe upon my privacy when it comes to money.

---

1   Dodge sometimes used the pen name "Gail Hamilton."

These convictions effectively undercut efforts to teach about giving. It becomes increasingly hard to mount persuasive arguments for giving if one doubts the possibility of arriving at shared and presumably authoritative standards that would guide all members of a community in their decision. The familiar question—By what authority?—clearly had not been put to rest.

The dominant theme of this period, however, was systematization. Like other modern organizations, especially the corporations, early twentieth-century denominations were caught up in the excitement of becoming large national institutions. Progress required efficiency, and efficiency required a new kind of church bureaucrat or manager. The old-style traveling financial agents passed off the scene. Now what was needed were experts who could help the churches become truly business-like in fund-raising. What was needed was system, method, and planning. "If a well-systematized financial plan can be presented in the local church," a northern Methodist Board declared in 1912, "we have confidence that the church will respond in generous measure." The congregations will respond only if everyone is educated in systematic giving. "That is a tremendous task," the Methodist bishops concurred, "but it must be undertaken. And the first step toward it is to find a rational, Scriptural, systematic basis for asking" (quoted in Primer 1979:71).

Several innovations had already taken root. Increasing numbers of congregations across denominational boundaries were asking members to make an annual pledge and to pay it in weekly installments. The Sunday collection was becoming a familiar rite. The "duplex" envelope for the weekly offering arrived on the church scene in the last decades of the nineteenth century. Still used in some Protestant congregations, this two-pocketed envelope allows the giver to divide the offering between current expenses of the local church and missions support. The envelope system afforded a measure of privacy, which had become increasingly important in all matters pertaining to money. "Whirlwind" campaigns to raise money for building projects came into vogue, thanks to the fund-raising efforts of the YMCA. The heart of these intensive, short-term campaigns was the activities of volunteers who would visit every prospective contributor. The notion of a campaign—another martial metaphor—served as the prototype for financial campaigns in twentieth-century organizations.

There was one crucial element missing in this emerging system. It lacked a name or a dominant symbol. The phrases "every-member canvass" or "systematic benevolence" could hardly serve as rallying cries for a new generation of church faithful. Denominational leaders chose "stewardship" as their new motto.

Stewardship became a popular metaphor for at least three reasons. First, it offered a relatively fresh way of talking about faith and money. Second, it had a biblical lineage. While the previous generation of church leaders had based their giving theology on the slender reed of one verse, I Corinthians 16:2, the stewardship enthusiasts could roam through the New Testament parables about stewards. Third, and perhaps most important, it blended nicely with the values of white middle-class America. The good steward was an effective manager in addition to being a faithful trustee. Stewards—whether of the first century or the twentieth—cherish order, efficiency, planning, and taking responsibility. The idea of a steward being a voluntary and generous giver, however, was a new idea.

The core message about stewardship offered three propositions: Christians are called to be stewards of what God has given them, the good steward cares for temporary possessions given in trust, and, not least, the good steward returns to God that portion of money required by Scripture. The final proposition presented a problem, for there was no common agreement on the *amount* that Scripture required the faithful to give.

In the later part of the nineteenth century, believers had been urged to give "as God has prospered them." This view of "proportionate" giving gradually fell into disfavor in the early part of the twentieth century. It offered, first of all, no specific guidance for hard decisions. How would church members know what their fair proportion was, apart from full and candid discussion with others? Moreover, open talk about money—especially when it exposed differences in income—threatened the egalitarian veneer of many American congregations.

There was another reason proportionate giving never became the prevailing version of the biblical "law" for giving. It had to compete with a revival of interest in the ancient practice of tithing. The newfound popularity of the tithe toward the end of the nineteenth century represented a surprising reversal of opinion among American Protestants. In previous decades, tithing had been the subject of fierce debates. Old memories of the tithe as a hated symbol of imposed religious taxes in Europe still lingered in some quarters.

In the early 1900s, a few passionate believers in tithing created the outward appearance of a popular movement sweeping the country. A flood of pamphlets and books, all aimed at reaching the average laymen, created a populist-like outcry against seminaries that were *not* teaching about tithing. While the seminaries and denominations taught in "generalities," the supporters of the tithe believed their teachings were specific, clear, and the embodiment of God's law. The tithe had mass appeal because it was simple to understand and because it required the same rate of payment from all people, rich or poor.

The impact of this tithing movement prompted stewardship pioneers in the 1920s to advocate tithing in the mainstream denominations. Tithing now became the necessary first step to fulfilling the Christian's duty toward God, and proportionate giving was for those few souls who willingly ventured beyond tithing. From the 1910s onward, stewardship became a cause that inspired loyalty as well as great expectations for the future. By the end of the decade, according to one of its leading interpreters, "the Stewardship Movement has increased from a trembling whisper in the desert to a commanding voice in the councils of the churches" (Calkins 1919:7).

One of the reasons for the meteoric rise of the stewardship movement was the institutional muscle of its founding generation. The church leaders constituting the stewardship movement were strategically placed bureaucrats who knew how to use denominational channels to reach a large population, and there was a ready audience in the hinterlands. Increasing numbers of congregations wanted to know how to run an every-member canvass, and there is always a hunger, when it comes to fund-raising, for fresh language and new techniques. The stewardship executives could supply manuals and tracts, recruit volunteers from across the country, arrange training sessions for them, and thereby create a national network that would lend credence to claims of an expanding movement.

The year 1919 marked the crest of optimism about fund-raising in the "mainstream" churches. A coalition of 30 denominations (representing about 60 percent of the Protestant population) were preparing to undertake one of the most ambitious financial challenges in the history of American Protestantism: the Interchurch World Movement. The goal of this movement was to raise more than one third of a billion dollars over a three-year period for home and foreign missions. The movement hoped to recruit millions of "stewards" who would assist in this effort, and each steward would carry a card that set forth the principles of stewardship:

> (1) God is the owner of all things; (2) Every man is a Steward and must give account for all that is entrusted to him; (3) God's ownership and men's stewardship ought to be acknowledged; (4) This acknowledgment requires . . . setting apart . . . such a portion of the income as is recognized by the individual to be the will of God. (Ernst 1974:108-109)

Notice that tithing is not mentioned.

After a year of intense preparation, the campaign opened on January 1, 1920. Within a few weeks, the Interchurch leaders knew they were in deep trouble. The population was more diffident than excited, and the Movement sank into debt at a dizzying rate. The final collapse came several months later. What looked so beguiling and heroic in 1919 dissolved into a humiliating embarrassment by the spring of 1920. The era of idealist and expansionist causes was over, and all American institutions were entering a desperate scramble for survival.

A LONG DRY SPELL:
1940s-PRESENT

Somewhere in the 1920s and 1930s, after years of wearing repetition, stewardship talk had begun to lose its appeal for some ministers. Although the ritual of a "Budget Sunday" seemed inevitable, some ministers quietly jettisoned the notion of stewardship or used it as merely a slogan for fund-raising. By mid-century, claims for a definitive Christian understanding of giving were on the wane, replaced by pleas for money to maintain the congregation or the institution of the church. The language of "support," and its close cousin, "development," was adopted by an increasing number of churches, while the words "sacrificial" and "systematic" were dropped. The nub of the new argument resided in a plea for loyalty: Give so that the church may remain intact and therefore ready to serve future generations. A plea for loyalty to an institution depends almost entirely, of course, upon the health and vitality of the particular institution in question.

In the decades between the two world wars many changes had taken place in American society. The federal income tax was now taking a sizable bite out of the incomes of middle-class families. At the same time, nonprofit organizations, such as the Red Cross and the Community Chest, competed with churches for voluntary donations. At this time the tithe was redefined by some church leaders. It was suggested that 5 percent of one's income (after taxes) go to other community agencies and 5 percent to one's church. This "modern" tithe never caught the imagination of most Protestants. For the conservative churches it was a watering down of the Old Testament standard of tithing 10 percent to the church. For those who advocated proportional giving it seemed like replacing one percentage figure with another.

By the 1960s and early 1970s, mainstream Protestants no longer found themselves in an era of church growth and expansion. There were tensions and divisions over civil rights and Vietnam, and denominational loyalty was often stretched to the breaking point. Money—raising it or teaching about it—became of secondary importance; the primary issue for the church was what it meant to live faithfully in the rapidly changing world. Institutional survival was taken for granted as churches and denominations were able to ride on the financial prosperity of the 1950s and 1960s.

The year 1973 marked a turning point for the churches. The long stretch of prosperity came to an end, Americans started facing double-digit inflation, and the hidden economic weaknesses of many mainline denominations became evident. Current receipts were not enough to maintain church institutions, which had burgeoned in the previous decades, and church investments and savings began to shrink alarmingly. Mainstream denominations and churches began to face an uncertain future, and reorganizations and retrenchments became regular cyclical events in many places. In response to this crisis, some denominational institutions—especially the colleges and seminaries—became more dependent upon the language and methods of the "development" industry.

In the early 1980s, a new voice brought hope and a challenge to the churches. Douglas John Hall, a Canadian theologian, published a series of lectures on stewardship, *The Steward: A Biblical Symbol Come of Age* (1982). Stewardship had become "embarrassing," he wrote, because it "conjures up the horrors of every-person visitations, building projects, financial campaigns, and the seemingly incessant harping of the churches for more money" (p. 6). Stewardship, properly understood, should encompass a vast array of responsibilities, and under its canopy one should include environmentalism, justice issues, and global problems. Hall's work dominated mainstream thinking about stewardship into the early 1990s; indeed *The Steward* became the most popular book on this subject since the early part of the century.

Despite all the claims for new insights, however, this flurry of excitement did not lead to any new interpretation of giving. A few denominations, such as the Episcopal Church, started to stress tithing in the 1980s, and while it had some success in this venture, it also brought a great deal of confusion. One person remarked at a vestry meeting, "So when the Bible talks about money, we're fundamentalists?" This sort of confusion reflected a deeper perplexity that had increasingly haunted mainstream churches during the past 20 years: By what authority do congregations make claims upon our money?

PRACTICAL CONCLUSIONS

So we are brought full circle. The words "financial crisis" echo up and down the corridors of power, and in this swirling vortex of change and fear the question of authority remains. Why give? It appears that four practical conclusions can be drawn from this historical overview of answers to this question.

1. Currently popular practices, and justifications for those practices, are historically variable rather than eternal. Religious leaders searching to persuade people to give to their congregations and causes might ponder, in this light, the arguments they offer in these appeals. Consider tithing, for example. Is tithing anything more than a church custom that has been much praised but only occasionally practiced? In what sense is it "God's law"? If tithing is just an optional custom, practiced in some eras and sharply criticized in others, then how can it be a part of our core convictions about giving?

2. "Stewardship," which once seemed to be a promising theological ideal upon which to base our giving, now means many different things to mainstream churchgoers. For some, it is a shorthand phrase that covers all dimensions of Protestant fund-raising. For others, it signifies a set of theological propositions, such as "God is the owner of all our possessions." For still others, it is the symbol of Christian responsibility for the environment, and, for a smaller group, it describes the essential unity of a Christian lifestyle. If stewardship means all these things, does it mean anything in particular? Can it carry any authority? Perhaps it is time to question whether or not "stewardship" can work as today's dominant metaphor justifying and legitimating financial contributions to churches and other religious organizations.

3. Stewardship educators have, traditionally, fought hard to distinguish between their high calling and the work of "development" experts. As a matter of fact, however, one cannot fully understand the unfolding story of stewardship and its predecessors apart from the exigencies of fund-raising. There is, and apparently always has been, an intimate and intricate relationship between theologies of giving and the pragmatic exigencies of fund-raising. The concept of sacrificial giving first became popular at a time of intense competition for funds among benevolent agencies. The concept of stewardship first became popular during a time of organization building and striving for efficiency. Religious leaders probably would benefit from a deeper appreciation of the relationship between theological teachings about giving, on the one hand, and pragmatic fund-raising activity, on the other hand.

4. The search began long ago for some authority that will make teachings about giving both believable and compelling. That search has generated a range of teachings that, if taken together, often present a confused and incoherent theological perspective. How, then, can religious organizations persuade their indifferent givers to become more generous? The historical

overview in this chapter strongly suggests that there is no obvious answer to this question. Perhaps the historical lesson is that there can be no single answer.

REFERENCES

Calkins, Harvey Reeves. 1919. "Introduction." In *Modern Stewardship Sermons by Representative Preachers,* edited by Ralph Cushman. New York and Cincinnati: Abingdon.

Ernst, Eldon G. 1974. *Moment of Truth for Protestant America: Interchurch Campaigns Following World War One.* Missoula, MT: American Academy of Religion and Scholar's Press. Dissertation Series, Number 3.

Hall, Douglas John. 1982. *The Steward: A Biblical Symbol Comes of Age.* New York: Friendship Press for Commission on Stewardship, National Council of the Churches of Christ in the U.S.A.

Hamilton, Gail. 1877. *Sermons to the Clergy.* Boston: Estes and Lauriat.

Harris, Samuel. 1850. *Zaccheus; or The Scriptural Plan of Benevolence.* New York: The American Tract Society.

Lynn, Robert Wood. 1995. *Why Give? Stewardship: A Documentary History of One Strand in American Protestant Teachings About Giving, 1825-1985.* Available from the author in diskette form: 22 Carroll Street, Portland, ME 04102.

Primer, Ben. 1979. *Protestant and American Business Methods.* Ann Arbor: UMI Research Press.

Chapter 8

The Crisis in
the Churches

ROBERT WUTHNOW

Financial woes are the order of the day in America's churches. Mission programs are being canceled. Homeless people are being turned away from soup kitchens because donations of time and money are too small. Pastors' salary increases are being postponed, sometimes for the fifth or sixth year in a row. Youth ministers are being dismissed. Music programs are being scaled back. Second and third calls are made to parishioners begging them to turn in their pledge cards. At denominational headquarters and in seminaries, church leaders are projecting cutbacks and austerity-level programs well into the next century.

It is tempting to assume that this crisis is *merely* financial. In fact, however, serious as these problems may be, they are nevertheless only the tip of an iceberg. Churches have weathered economic hardship before. During the Great Depression, for example, many churches postponed putting up new buildings and went without permanent, full-time staff for more than a decade, but by the early 1950s most had recovered financially and were expanding their programs to meet the challenges of growing numbers of church

AUTHOR'S NOTE: This chapter is adapted from *The Crisis in the Churches: Spiritual Malaise, Fiscal Woe,* by Robert Wuthnow. Copyright 1997 by Robert Wuthow; used by permission of Oxford University Press, Inc.

members. Were the present crisis only a problem of budgets, careful management would be enough, but the current crisis is much deeper. Fund-raisers cannot fix it.

The basic thesis of this chapter is that the current financial crisis is, in fact, a *spiritual crisis*. The problem lies less in parishioners' pocketbooks than in their hearts and less in churches' budgets than in clergy's understanding of the needs and desires of their members' lives. It lies in a fundamental unwillingness on the part of clergy to confront the teachings within their own confessional heritage. The prevalent theology seldom connects with the ways in which people think about their money or their work, and when it does, the connection is more likely to be one of solace than of prophetic vision.

The crisis pertains most directly to the middle class. For all its interest in the poor, the church in the United States is overwhelmingly a ministry to the middle class. Its programs are geared toward the interests of middle-class families. It depends on the middle class for its financial existence. Its members mostly lead comfortable middle-class lives and make up the majority of one of the richest countries in the world.

Church members also suffer from the pressures to which middle-class families are increasingly exposed—pressures of working harder to make ends meet, worries about retaining one's job, lack of time for one's self and one's family, marital strains associated with two-career households, and the incessant demands of advertising and the marketplace. These are the daily preoccupations of the middle class, yet clergy have often been reluctant to acknowledge these issues as legitimate concerns or to address them seriously. Especially in recent years, it has seemed more pressing to take up the issues supplied by the media and to become embroiled in culture wars and preach about politics rather than speak to the concerns that face parishioners in their everyday lives.

Because they do not find clergy who are concerned about the pressures they face in their families and at work, it is not surprising that many middle-class people are giving proportionately less to their church than they were a decade or two ago. They may still attend services on Sunday mornings, but they receive little guidance about how to be faithful stewards. In fact, most of them have no idea what stewardship is. Church members are unlikely to consider their work a calling or to approach it any differently than their less devout neighbors. They may consider it as legitimate to give money to the Sierra Club as to the Presbyterian church, and they may turn to Alcoholics Anonymous to find help in coping with the pressures of daily existence because the pastor seems incapable of listening to their problems.

This chapter describes the spiritual condition of the middle class when it comes to work and money, and it documents how difficult it is for the clergy to speak effectively to that condition. I argue that the church's financial crisis in fact stems from a general failure on the part of churches and clergy to speak to the real economic concerns of the American middle class. This argument is supported by data gathered from scores of churches throughout the United States, representing most major confessional and denominational traditions. Both clergy and laity were interviewed in depth, and more than 200 sermons were examined to see how clergy perceive and speak to the issues facing them and their congregants. I also draw on data collected from a survey of a representative national sample of working men and women.

In this chapter, it is possible only to sketch the outlines of the spiritual crisis to which I point. Readers interested in more substance and detail should see the book from which this chapter is adapted (Wuthnow 1997).

THE SPIRITUAL DILEMMA
OF THE MIDDLE CLASS

The most notable source of pressure for the middle class is simply the increasing number of hours that people are having to work. According to one study, the average American now puts in a total of about *one full month* more on the job per year than was true a generation ago (Schor 1991). Not counted in this estimate is the fact that more and more people are employed in professional occupations in which evening and weekend work is common and that most women are now gainfully employed outside the home, whereas this was not the case a generation ago. At present, two thirds of all church members who are employed at all work more than 40 hours a week, and one church member in six works more than 50 hours a week. Sixty-five percent say they are working harder now than they were five years ago.

The vast majority of church members are glad to be working, of course. They take pride in their jobs and derive much of their self-esteem from performing well at their work. Indeed, 82 percent say that their work is a very important source of their self-identity. Yet a large number of church members also are concerned about how much they have to work. They are faced with serious pressures, work-related stress, and too little time to do the things they really want to do. Seventy percent say they have little or no energy left over for other things when they come home from work, 50 percent wish they could work fewer hours than they do, and 50 percent say they should be getting more sleep than they do. In all, 53 percent of church members who are working full- or part-time say they experience significant amounts of stress at their jobs at least once a week.

Added to these concerns are the growing problems associated with balancing work commitments and family commitments. These problems are especially significant among parents, including the growing number of working women or single mothers, who work long hours to support their families and then have little time to spend with them. A substantial minority of church members say they have experienced trouble arranging for child care, getting household tasks done, or juggling schedules with busy spouses. A majority (56 percent) also admit that bad days at work make them cranky with their families.

How well do the churches minister to these needs? Judging from what people report, not well. One indication is what people do to relieve stress that develops at work. Only about a quarter of church members (28 percent) say they routinely pray or meditate. Scarcely anyone (4 percent) talks to his or her pastor. The most common strategies for dealing with stress are to watch television, get some physical exercise, or go shopping. Those who attend religious services every week are almost as likely as those who attend less often to say they are dissatisfied with their work and to complain of burnout. They are also just as likely to report that one of their favorite ways of dealing with job-related stress is to go shopping. Even if a major ethical dilemma arose at work, only 13 percent said they would talk to their pastor about it, compared with 54 percent who say they would discuss the problem with their boss, 36 percent who say they would talk it over with co-workers, and 20 percent who would find something helpful to read.

Work and money are closely related, of course, but financial pressures take on a life of their own, creating anxieties that are often only partly attributable to what kind of job one has. The bottom line for most middle-class families is that they feel severely pressured financially. Seventy percent of employed church members say they have been worried in the past year about how to pay their bills. Nearly this many (59 percent) also say they think a lot about money and their personal finances. Moreover, many people experience anxiety from having to make hard decisions about how to use their money. Specifically, 72 percent of church members with jobs say they have been bothered during the past year by anxiety about purchases or other decisions involving money, and a majority (52 percent) say they have felt guilty about the way they spent their money. Those who attend religious services every week are only slightly less likely than those who attend less often to say they would like to have a lot more money and to admit that they worry a lot about their finances, and the two groups are also nearly the same in saying that they value having a beautiful home, a new car, and other nice things. It would appear that the churches are not making a strong difference in the financial aspects of most people's lives.

At the same time, there is evidence that large segments of the middle class would like to forge deeper connections between their economic lives and their spiritual lives. Among church members with jobs, 71 percent say they want more out of life than just a good job and a comfortable lifestyle. More than a third (35 percent) feel they need more time to think about the really basic issues of life, and more than half (53 percent) say they would like to spend more time exploring spiritual issues. Yet it is unclear that the churches are helping people to think through the issues they really want to think through. In their opinions about a variety of aspects concerning the character of our society, active churchgoers do not differ significantly from the less active.

The middle class, then, is caught in a spiritual dilemma. On the one hand, it enjoys enormous resources—education, job training, places to live, food on the table, longevity, relative freedom from fear and violence. On the other hand, it feels overburdened with too much work and too many bills; it suffers stress and anxiety; it wonders what its values should be and wishes it could cut back and get its life more under control; it even recognizes the need to think about spiritual concerns. Faced with this dilemma, the middle class turns in large numbers to the churches to find help. Yet the churches don't seem to be making much of a difference in the economic aspects of middle-class lives.

WHAT THE CLERGY ARE SAYING

If there is a problem in the churches, it is not because pastors fail to recognize the importance of economic matters both for the financial health of their ministries and as concerns in the lives of their parishioners. Their theological training convinces clergy that faith in God should have implications for all of life, including the work people do and the ways in which they spend their money. Pastors emphasize that people of faith should be especially responsible in the decisions they make, work harder and longer than other people, spend their money wisely, and be diligent in supporting the church. This emphasis resonates strongly with the norms of economic responsibility that already pervade the American middle class.

Clergy also are at least partly attuned to the spiritual dilemma that arises from the pressures under which middle America exists. Many pastors are aware of how little free time their members have. Pastors understand that parishioners may not have energy to attend church meetings or do volunteer work. Pastors are also keenly aware of the pressures that encourage church members to spend money on material pleasures, even to the point of going heavily into debt. Most pastors, after all, are themselves members of the middle class. They live in middle-class neighborhoods, have working spouses, and are raising children amid the present culture of overconsumption. They are also overwhelmed by these issues. Faced with the task of providing leadership, they instead admit to feeling frustrated, feeling guilty for doing too little, and feeling uncertain about how to be more effective.

The clergy with whom we spoke uniformly regarded the economic realm as an important area of ministry. Unlike the laypeople we considered, pastors believe firmly that work and money should not be placed in a separate compartment from spirituality, but that economic behavior should be decisively influenced by a person's faith. In the view of most, economic behavior symbolizes an individual's priorities and thus their spiritual health. Pastors argue that individuals should take responsibility for establishing an appropriate perspective on work, talents, and money—seeing them as divine gifts rather than individual accomplishments. A responsible individual should, therefore, draw a large number of connections between the spiritual and the economic aspects of his or her life. This means taking economic responsibility for their own families; caring for individuals in their immediate circle of acquaintances who may be in need; and, by extension, playing a responsible role in supporting the church to which they belong.

As this last sentence implies, most pastors are candid in admitting that economic issues are especially important to them because the financial welfare of their congregations depends on how those issues are resolved. When asked what sorts of connection they would like to see their members making between faith and economic matters, many pastors jumped immediately to a discussion of religious giving.

Many pastors feel that what they have to say or teach about money makes little difference in their parishioners' lives because they are up against an entire economic and cultural system. They also feel that their parishioners are genuinely too busy with life to listen to their admonitions, let alone take them seriously. They also feel frustrated in addressing economic matters because they sense that people don't want the pastor to meddle in their financial affairs. Consequently, many pastors feel they have no sense of how much their congregants earn or where their money goes. Even some of those pastors who did feel they knew about their members' economic lives seemed to be operating in the dark, giving very inaccurate estimates of their members' incomes.

Many pastors admitted that they had done little to motivate their congregants to relate their faith to the economic realm. Others said they had done a little but felt they didn't understand the issues well enough or have the time to do more. In several cases, clergy were genuinely intimidated by the subject. In other cases, clergy whittle down the issue to more manageable proportions by focusing the bulk of their attention on giving and church finances. Asked what they are doing to encourage parishioners to relate the two realms, they turn immediately to their favorite fund-raising techniques. Other pastors take a much wider view of what must be done to apply Christian principles to economic issues but do so in a way that makes the task truly intimidating. Discussions of economic justice, in particular, seem to follow this path.

On the whole, pastors' sense of efficacy in addressing economic issues is quite low. As moral leaders, they betray doubt and uncertainty. They feel little authority to speak about concrete issues other than church finances. The image they present is of a weak voice surrounded by a vast sea of obstacles. In our survey of working Americans, 32 percent of church members said they had heard a sermon on the relationship between faith and personal finances in the last year, but both from talking with clergy about what they say and from examining the transcripts of their sermons, we must say that clergy often tiptoe around the topic of money as if they were taking a walk through a minefield. One of the most common ways of doing so is to sneak up on the topic like an adolescent hoping to steal a quick kiss in the dark without getting caught. A common approach is simply to remind worshipers that God gives us all that we have, then one can pray a kind of blanket prayer—"Thank you, God, for all our blessings"—and not have to say much more about money.

The clergy who are struggling most seriously with questions of money are often concerned, above all, with getting people to see it in relation to the rest of their lives, especially their values. Two thirds (68 percent) of the working public agree that money is one thing; morals and values are completely separate. Church members are just as likely as nonmembers to take this view. The challenge for clergy is to start breaking down this wall between the economic world and the spiritual and moral world.

PRACTICAL CONCLUSIONS

For the churches to regain their spiritual voice in ministering to the middle class, the clergy must play a key role. They must provide leadership and inspiration. They must preserve the sacred teachings of their traditions, making them relevant to the strenuous, pressure-filled lives that most of their middle-class parishioners lead. They must communicate effectively in their preaching and serve as role models in the ways that they lead their own lives. They must understand that middle-class people are much more concerned about how to work responsibly and how to manage their money wisely than they are about the propriety or impropriety of a Robert Mapplethorpe photograph. The clergy must do a better job of relating theology to everyday life, and they must realize that everyday life consists mostly of the work that people do in their ordinary jobs, not the work they do for an hour or two a week in the church basement. Pastors must preach more clearly and imaginatively about stewardship. They must give their members better reasons to contribute to the church, and they must help the middle class understand the relevance of faith in the workplace and the marketplace.

There are four practical ways that clergy might strive to address this spiritual crisis and thereby address the financial crisis.

1. First, clergy might talk more about money. All the pastors we talked to who had found it possible to preach about money did so, above all, because they took the subject seriously. They recognized that money matters to virtually everyone and that sound teaching about personal finances is part of the church's responsibility. When clergy made a pointed effort to speak to financial issues, they often encouraged both financial responsibility and generosity, and they often challenged the implicit gospel of wealth that still prevails in middle-class culture.

Such preaching may well be more valuable and effective than clergy think. Among regularly attending church members, approximately a third of those who had heard a sermon about personal finances in the past year said they had also thought a great deal in the past year about what the Bible teaches concerning money and about the relationship between religious values and their personal finances. In comparison, fewer than a fifth of those who had not heard a sermon about personal finances had thought this much about these issues. Also, although most church members (even those who attend regularly) do not seek out their pastors to talk about financial concerns, the percentage who do so is considerably higher among those who have heard a sermon on finances: 10 percent versus 2 percent. Among church members who attend services at least once a week, giving was substantially higher among those who had heard a stewardship sermon within the past year than among those who had not heard a sermon on this topic.

A few sermons about finances are not going to challenge middle-class church members to lead their lives in fundamentally different ways, but these results suggest that the churches *can* make a difference.

2. In addition to preaching and talking, churches might be more pastorally active in ministering to the economic concerns of middle-class parishioners, helping them to understand their work as ministry, to cope with stress and burnout, to keep their priorities straight with respect to money, and to manage their resources with greater care. This might be done in various ways. Clergy might include discussions of money in the pastoral counseling they do with couples planning to be married. Seminars might be held in the church to address specific financial concerns about, for example, budgeting, keeping records of major purchases, working out disagreements with friends or relatives concerning money, avoiding impulse buying, learning to do comparison shopping, waiting for sales, locating secondhand items, making safe investments, avoiding high interest payments, and so on. By sponsoring such events or classes, the church can demonstrate to its members the importance of finances and the relevance of faith to these issues.

3. More generally, churches can be places where personal, practical, ongoing discussions of money can take place. Small groups are an especially promising setting in which members might discuss work, personal finances, and stewardship, among other topics, and hold each other accountable in these areas. The advantages of small groups are considerable. They cost relatively little to operate; leadership is generally drawn from the laity and from members who have already benefited from participation in groups; study guides and other materials can be obtained readily and inexpensively in almost any subject on which groups wish to focus; small groups provide intimate and informal interaction that can be the basis for sharing concerns about work, money, or other personal issues; and these groups can focus on practical applications of faith to the concerns of everyday life. Finances are one of the hardest issues for churchgoers to discuss candidly, even in small groups. Leaders, however, can guide small groups, even behind the scenes, and clergy often stimulate small-group discussions, perhaps more than they realize, by the sermons they preach.

4. Tough-minded churches also need to be aware of the *institutional* realities that govern contemporary life. Middle-class parishioners may not be able to work fewer than 50 hours a week, because their employers insist on such effort. Their employers, in turn, may think the only way to compete effectively is by squeezing more hours of work from their employees without paying them any more. These employers may not have considered other

factors—such as burnout and employee turnover—or other options—such as part-time and contract work. Churches that simply tell individual members to work less and enjoy themselves more are unlikely to have much of an impact on such circumstances. Churches that work with local business councils to consider institutional alternatives are likely to make more of a difference. Engaging in discussion of such institutional change is another way churches might prove themselves relevant to the real concerns that animate their middle-class members in everyday life.

REFERENCES

Schor, Juliet B. 1991. *The Overworked American*. New York: Basic Books.
Wuthnow, Robert. 1997. *The Crisis in the Churches: Spiritual Malaise, Fiscal Woe*. New York: Oxford University Press.

PART II

CONGREGATIONS AND RESOURCES

Chapter **9**

Financing Religious Congregations

A National View

VIRGINIA HODGKINSON

This chapter is based on the results of a 1992 national survey of congregations, conducted by Independent Sector (IS). The sample for this
study was drawn from the approximately 257,000 religious congregations
listed in the Yellow Pages published by the nation's telephone companies. It
consists of five stratified random samples, each of 1,003 congregations.
These samples were stratified both by region and by urban/rural location.
Every 250th congregation was sampled, and then four additional "shadow"
samples were drawn to supplement this initial sample. The shadow sampling
technique was selected in order to assure a response rate of at least 60 percent. Overall, 3,779 congregations were asked to participate in the study, and
727 usable surveys (19 percent) were returned. These completed surveys
covered 615 (61.5 percent) of the original 1,003 sampling units.

AUTHOR'S NOTE: This chapter is adapted from *From Belief to Commitment: The Community Service Activities and Finances of Religious Congregations in the United States, 1993
Edition*, by Virginia A. Hodgkinson and Murray S. Weitzman. © 1992 by Independent Sector,
Washington, DC.; used with permission. See Appendix A of that report for more detail about
the shadow sampling technique.

TABLE 9.1 Congregations' Human Resources

	All Congregations	Small Congregations	Medium Congregations	Large Congregations
Percentage of congregations with at least one full-time paid clergyperson	88	70	90	97
Percentage of congregations with two or more full-time paid clergypersons	20	4	8	53
Percentage of congregations with at least one volunteer clergyperson	19	25	18	17
Percentage of congregations with at least one full-time paid employee other than clergy	29	4	20	64
Percentage of congregations with at least one part-time paid employee other than clergy	62	32	60	88
Average number of volunteers in an average month	53	20	37	109
Percentage of congregations using at least 15 volunteers in an average month	83	56	85	96

The survey investigated the full range of congregational activities, as well as their participation in the larger community. This chapter is limited to an overview of results related to the resources and expenditure patterns of congregations. Readers interested in more details about substantive results should see Hodgkinson and Weitzman (1992), from which this chapter is adapted.

CONGREGATIONAL RESOURCES

The IS survey collected data on two aspects of congregational resources: people and finances. Table 9.1 gives the basic results regarding congregations' human resources. Here, as throughout this chapter, results are presented both for the congregational population as a whole and also separately for small, medium, and large congregations. Small congregations (20 percent of the sample) are those with fewer than 100 members or attendees. Medium congregations (52 percent of the sample) have between 100 and 399 members or attendees. Large congregations (28 percent of the sample) have 400 or more members or attendees.

Congregations were asked to report both the number of paid clergy they employed and the number of paid employees other than clergy. As Table 9.1 shows, the vast majority of congregations in this sample (88 percent) have at least one full-time paid clergyperson. Although small congregations are less likely than either medium or large congregations to have a full-time paid clergyperson, almost three quarters (70 percent) of the smallest congregations employ a full-time clergyperson. The effect of size on a congregation's likelihood of employing additional staff, however, is substantial. Fewer than 10 percent of small or medium-sized congregations have two or more full-time clergy, compared with more than half (53 percent) of the large congregations. Similar dramatic differences are present when it comes to full- and part-time staff other than clergy, although about one third (32 percent) of the small congregations employ at least one part-time paid employee other than clergy.

Congregations depend heavily on volunteers as well as on paid clergy and other staff. The average number of volunteers per congregation was 53. The average number of volunteers at small congregations was 20; at medium-size congregations, 37; and at large congregations, 109. Eighty-three percent of all congregations use at least 15 volunteers in an average month. The importance of volunteers to the human resource base of congregations is especially apparent when we calculate the relative contributions of clergy, paid employees, and volunteers. Overall, 89 percent of people engaged in working at congregations were volunteers. Of course, paid clergy and other staff work more hours, but volunteer labor remains a substantial part of the human resource base even in terms of number of hours worked. Overall, clergy provide 25 percent of the total hours worked at congregations. The work done by paid employees represented 29 percent, and the work of volunteers constituted 47 percent of total work hours.

Turning to financial resources, the total revenue for the average congregation in this sample was $188,000. Data on congregations' revenue streams are presented in Table 9.2. It is clear that congregations derive most of their income from individual giving. Overall, the average congregation receives 86

TABLE 9.2 Congregations' Revenue Streams

	All Congregations	Small Congregations	Medium Congregations	Large Congregations
Average percentage of congregational revenue from:				
Individual giving	81	82	83	80
Other contributions	5	6	5	5
Program revenue	14	12	12	15
Average percentage of individual giving via:				
Pledges	39	21	34	43
Collections	59	78	64	54
Fixed fees	2	1	1	3
Percentage of congregations receiving no income				
from pledges	55	69	55	47
from collections	8	9	7	8
from fixed fees	91	95	91	89

percent of its income from individual giving or other contributions (bequests, contributions from denominational organizations, charities, etc.). Interestingly, this dependence on contributions, and especially individual contributions, does not vary much by size of congregation.

There is variation, however, in the extent to which congregations derive their individual contributions via a pledge system—a system by which individuals promise to give a specific dollar amount in a given year—and the extent to which individual donations came, without pledges, via the collection plate. Overall, the average congregation received 39 percent of its individual contributions via pledges, but this amount varies from 21 percent for small congregations to 43 percent for large congregations. Fewer than half (47 percent) of the large congregations receive no income from pledges, compared with 69 percent of small congregations. Fixed fees (including membership dues) are an important revenue source for only a small percentage of religious congregations. Although the religious affiliation of congregations is not available in the IS data set, it seems likely that Jewish synagogues, in which membership dues are a common financing practice, account for some proportion of the 9 percent of congregations receiving at least some income from fixed fees.

TABLE 9.3 Congregations' Expenditures

	All Congregations	Small Congregations	Medium Congregations	Large Congregations
Average percentage of congregational expenditures for:				
Salaries, benefits, and professional fees	44	46	45	43
Property, construction, capital improvements, and occupancy costs	27	30	26	27
Other current operating costs	12	11	12	12
Donations within the denomination	10	6	9	10
Donations to nondenominational organizations and direct assistance to individuals	4	4	3	5
Savings	4	3	4	4

CONGREGATIONAL EXPENDITURES

Just as congregations' income is dominated by contributions from individuals, congregations' expenditures are dominated by local operating costs. Table 9.3 presents the basic results. On average, congregations spend 83 percent of their financial resources on local operations: 44 percent for personnel (salaries, benefits, etc.), 27 percent for building-related expenses (property acquisition, capital improvements, and occupancy costs), and 12 percent for other operating costs. Interestingly, this breakdown does not vary much by size of congregation. Congregations direct, on average, 4 percent of their spending either to direct assistance to individuals or to charitable organizations outside the denomination. This may sound like a small amount, but readers should note that 4 percent of congregational expenditures amounts to approximately $2 billion per year in charitable giving by congregations. This amount is even larger when we assign value to the volunteer time mobilized by congregations.

TABLE 9.4 Percentage of Congregations Using Various Fund-Raising Strategies

Strategy	All Congregations	Small Congregations	Medium Congregations	Large Congregations
Make extensive use of board members in fund-raising	30	12	30	43
Develop a long-range strategy to increase individual giving	26	11	27	34
Make use of special events like carnivals, dinners, etc.	24	18	25	27
Give existing staff fund-raising responsibility	23	16	22	30
Make use of sales of products such as T-shirts, bake sales, etc.	18	15	20	20
Fees or user charges	12	4	11	20
Hire an outside fund-raising specialist	6	1	5	11
Obtain support from foundations or corporate sponsors	4	2	4	5
Obtain support from government programs	1	0	1	3
Set up profit-making subsidiary	1	0	2	1
Seek membership in United Way or other federated charities	1	1	1	1
Hire a fund-raising staff person	1	0	1	1

This amount is even larger when we assign value to the volunteer time mobilized by congregations.

CONGREGATIONAL FUND-RAISING STRATEGIES

Congregations were given a set of fund-raising strategies and asked if any of them were in place. Table 9.4 gives the results. The five fund-raising strategies most commonly reported were making extensive use of board members in fund-raising (30 percent); developing a long-range strategy to increase individual giving (26 percent); using special events like carnivals or dinners (24 percent); giving existing staff responsibility for fund-raising (23 percent); and using sales of products such as T-shirts and baked goods (18 percent). Very few congregations hire outside fund-raising specialists, set up profit-making subsidiaries, or obtain support from foundations, corporations, or government programs.

Unlike the basic patterns of revenue sources and expenditures, there are substantial differences between small, medium, and large congregations when it comes to fund-raising strategies. Overall, larger congregations use more strategies. In particular, they seem much more likely to use their board members for fund-raising, to have long-term strategies in place, and to hire outside fund-raising specialists.

PRACTICAL CONCLUSIONS

Five practical conclusions emerge from this overview.

1. Size matters to congregational financing and resource patterns, but in complex ways. Small congregations are not much different than large congregations when it comes to dependence on individual giving or on the proportion that is spent on local operating costs. One way that small congregations are substantially different from large congregations, however, is in the presence of paid staff—both clergy and lay. Religious leaders should be aware of the relative scarcity of paid staff in small and even medium-sized congregations, and they should recognize the constraints that small staffs place on implementing programs of various sorts.

2. Congregations of all sizes depend enormously on volunteer labor to carry out their work. Recognizing the importance of volunteers to congregations—along with the opportunities and constraints of such reliance—may help religious leaders to design more appropriate financial and management strategies for their congregations.

3. Virtually all congregations rely on individual donations as their primary funding stream. Religious leaders are well aware of the opportunities and challenges presented by such dependence. They may be less aware that relying completely on individual donations is a choice that congregations make, and one that need not be considered unalterable. Congregations relied on other sources of funding at earlier points in American history (see Chapter

3. Virtually all congregations rely on individual donations as their primary funding stream. Religious leaders are well aware of the opportunities and challenges presented by such dependence. They may be less aware that relying completely on individual donations is a choice that congregations make, and one that need not be considered unalterable. Congregations relied on other sources of funding at earlier points in American history (see Chapter 6), and alternative funding streams—bequests, endowments, foundation support, corporate support, government support for social service activities, and so on—may be available to some congregations. Congregational leaders need not feel trapped by their current dependence on individual donations.

4. Some research (see Chapter 1) suggests that pledge systems generate higher levels of giving than systems that rely on spontaneous donations when the collection plate is passed. A majority (55 percent) of congregations in this sample still do not use a pledge system, suggesting that there may be room for increased use of pledges among congregations, especially among small congregations.

5. It seems that congregations—and, again, especially small congregations—may underuse fund-raising strategies that have been successfully employed in other nonprofit organizations. Not every strategy, of course, is appropriate for every congregation, but it seems likely that congregations could benefit from considering strategies such as making more extensive use of board members for fund-raising, developing long-range strategies, using special events, and seeking support from foundations, corporations, and government programs.

REFERENCE

Hodgkinson, Virginia A., and Murray S. Weitzman. 1992. *From Belief to Commitment: The Community Service Activities and Finances of Religious Congregations in the United States, 1993 Edition.* Washington, DC: Independent Sector.

Chapter 10

Endowed Congregations

DEAN R. HOGE
LOREN B. MEAD

Church endowments have been, and still are, the source of much controversy. In addition to normative theological issues raised by endowments (e.g., is it appropriate for Christian churches to accumulate wealth?), there also are empirical questions. How many congregations have endowments? How much wealth is there in these endowments? What impact, if any, do endowments have on member giving? What investment decisions and strategies do churches make? How wisely are endowments managed? How important is theology in decisions about investing endowment funds and using the income that is generated? What are the correlations, if any, among the size of a church's endowment, its dependence on its endowment, and the giving behavior of its congregation?

In order to explore some of these issues, the National Association of Endowed Presbyterian Churches (NAEPC) asked us to conduct a study of how endowed Presbyterian churches manage, use, and view their invested funds. To do this, we developed a sample of endowed Presbyterian churches. Using denominational sources, we identified congregations with endowments over $500,000. We then constructed a sample that included 100 percent of the 95 Presbyterian congregations with invested funds greater than

$2.5 million and a randomly selected 70 percent of the 377 churches with endowments between $500,000 and $2.5 million. Contacting these congregations revealed that many of these churches in fact had invested funds less than $500,000. These congregations were removed from the study, resulting in a sample of 257 Presbyterian churches. We collected data from 142 of these churches, for a response rate of 55 percent. This sample, then, should be understood as a sample of Presbyterian churches with endowments greater than $500,000.

We also conducted focus group sessions in five different endowed congregations, each of which had invested funds ranging from $1 million to $5 million. In each of these churches, we met for a two-hour conversation with between six and 12 congregational leaders. Readers interested in more detail about our methods and findings should consult the longer report from which this chapter is adapted (Hoge and Mead 1995).

FINDINGS

Before we describe the findings from our study, it is important to emphasize the sheer amount of wealth held by Presbyterian churches in the United States. The Presbyterian Foundation holds investment management accounts and endowments for churches and other Presbyterian organizations. In 1995, these accounts and endowments totaled approximately $400 million dollars (Carr 1995). This amount, which reflects only that held by the Presbyterian Foundation, is surely an underestimate of the total wealth of Presbyterian churches. Only 9 percent of the churches in our sample, for example, were involved with the Presbyterian Foundation. Given that the median endowment for the 142 churches in our sample was $1.5 million, it seems plausible to conclude that the amount of wealth held by Presbyterian churches in the United States is on the order of *half a billion dollars*.

In this context, the characteristics of churches with invested funds perhaps take on increased significance. Among the basic facts emerging from our data are these:

- The median endowment for the 142 churches was $1.5 million, and 14 percent of the churches had over $5 million in invested funds.
- On average, 26 percent of a church's total expenditure was supported by endowment funds. (The median was 21 percent.)

- On average, 43 percent of endowment assets were invested in bonds; 42 percent in equities; 10 percent in money markets, CDs, or cash equivalents; 2 percent in real estate; and 2 percent in other financial instruments.

- A legal entity separate from the church controlled 22 percent of the endowments.

- Eighty-one percent (81 percent) of the churches had received gifts of $10,000 or more during the past three years. The vast majority of these gifts were bequests.

- Eighty-nine percent (89 percent) of the churches used endowment funds for their operating budget, 77 percent for mission and outreach, 68 percent for capital expenditures, and 51 percent for other specific purposes.

- The higher the percentage of endowment assets in bonds, the lower the total return percentage, and the higher the percentage of assets in equities, the higher the total return percentage.

- The vast majority of these churches—about 90 percent—regularly communicate to the congregation the amount and use both of the endowment principal and of the endowment income.

- Virtually all of these endowments—98 percent—were in urban or suburban churches.

- Sixty-five percent of these churches have a written policy concerning management, investment, and use of endowment principal and income.

- Twenty-four percent have a written policy concerning socially responsible investment of endowment funds.

Although our study focuses only on churches with relatively large endowments, there still is substantial range in this sample when it comes both to endowment size and to the extent to which a congregation depends on its endowment for annual expenditures. This variation allows us to examine the relationships among endowment size, congregational dependence on its endowment, and other variables of interest. Readers should bear in mind that the relationships reported here should not be generalized to the population of all Presbyterian congregations. That is, these results do not imply what might happen if a congregation with no endowment started to build one. Instead, these results should be understood as concerning only congregations that already have a fairly sizable endowment. The questions addressed in the tables presented here are of the form, *Among congregations with endowments of at least $500,000,* what are the effects of size and dependence on a variety of factors? Readers also should note that the bivariate relationships reported here may be explained by other factors, such as church location, size of congregation, and so on.

Small endowment churches (64 percent of the sample) were defined as those churches with invested funds of $2 million or less. Medium endow-

TABLE 10.1 Relationship Between Endowment Size and Selected Characteristics

	Endowment Size		
	Small $500,000 to $2,000,000 n = 91	Medium $2,000,001 to $5,000,000 n = 31	Large $5,000,001 to $41,000,000 n = 20
As endowment size increases:			
The average size of the church congregation increases	625	966	1,723
The percentage of churches in urban settings increases	31	45	65
The average percentage of church expenditure supported by the endowment increases	21	31	38
The average annual giving per member increases	$458	$477	$565
The percentage of churches with in-house management decreases	38	10	3
The percentage of churches with written policies concerning the management of funds increases	60	68	85
The percentage of churches with written policies concerning socially responsible investment of funds increases	14	33	50
The average percentage of endowment assets in equities increases	38	46	53
The average percentage of the endowment market value earned by interest and dividends decreases.	6.0	5.3	4.3
The average percentage of the endowment market value distributed from the endowment decreases	7.7	6.8	5.6

SOURCE: Adapted from Hoge & Mead, 1995; used with permission.

ment churches (22 percent) had invested funds between $2,000,001 and $5 million. Large endowment churches (14 percent of the sample) had invested funds of more than $5 million. The largest invested fund in this sample was $41 million. Table 10.1 shows the characteristics of congregations in these three endowment-size categories.

Churches with larger endowments have more members, are more urban, depend more on endowment income for annual expenditures, and have *higher* giving per member. They are less likely to manage their funds in-house, and they are more likely to have written policies concerning both management of the funds in general and concerning socially responsible investment policies. Perhaps related to fund management outside the congregation, larger endowments have higher percentages invested in equities. Importantly, in all three size categories, the average percentage distributed from the endowment is *higher* than the average percentage earned by endowments.[1]

Congregations with endowments vary widely in the extent to which they depend on those endowments to pay their bills. Another way to slice the pie is to examine how congregations with different levels of dependence on their endowments differ from one another. We broke the sample into three categories. Low support churches (31 percent of the sample) were defined as those that depend on their endowment for 12 percent or less of their total annual expenditure. Medium support churches (36 percent) depend on their endowments for 12.1 percent to 31 percent of their total expenditure. High support churches (33 percent of the sample) depend on their endowment for 31.1 percent to 90 percent of their total expenditure. The median level of support from endowments in this sample is 21 percent. Table 10.2 contains our findings on differences among congregations on this dimension.

Congregations that depend more on their invested funds are smaller, more urban, and have *lower* per member giving. They are less likely to manage these funds themselves, less likely to have written policies about using endowment income, but more likely to have written policies about socially responsible investment. As in Table 10.1, in all three categories, the percentage of endowment market value that is distributed is *higher than* the percentage earned in income. Interestingly, the more a congregation depends on its endowment income, the more likely it is to have endowment issues that are troubling to church leaders.

Our focus group discussions also yielded interesting insights on the ways congregations manage and think about their endowments. First, it seems that there is substantial variation in how congregational endowments come to be established. Some endowments began with one sudden large gift; others were the result of hard work and planning and came from numerous increments over a long period of time. Some endowments arrived with tight restrictions and specific designations; others did not. Some funds were given to outsiders (often local banks) to hold in trust for the congregation, giving the congregation's leaders discretion only in use of the income. In other churches, the congregation's leaders made all the decisions—from where the funds

---

1 A definitional ambiguity should be mentioned here. If congregations report only dividends, and not appreciation of the portfolio, as the "income" from an endowment, then the fact that, on average, the "percentage earned" is lower than the "percentage of market value distributed" may not represent a "spending down" of the endowment.

TABLE 10.2   Relationships Between Congregational Dependence on
Endowment and Selected Characteristics

	Level of Support From Endowment		
	Low 0-12% n = 44	Medium 12.1%-31% n = 51	High 31.1%-100% n = 47
As congregational dependence on endowments increases:			
The average size of the congregation decreases	1,095	891	588
Percentage of churches in urban settings increases	23	31	62
The average annual giving per member decreases	$538	$462	$440
The percentage of churches with in-house management decreases	32	31	19
The percentage of churches with written policies concerning the use of income from endowment funds decreases	82	63	53
The percentage of churches with written policies concerning socially responsible investment of funds increases	12	24	34
The average percentage of the endowment market value earned by interest and dividends was:	5.3	5.9	5.5
The average percentage of the endowment market value distributed from the endowment was:	5.4	8.6	7.3
The percentage of churches that had endowment issues that were troubling to their church leaders increases	46	61	76

SOURCE: Adapted from Hoge & Mead, 1995; used with permission.

would be held to how they were managed and what was to be done with
income and principal. It seems from just these five focus groups that there is
a great deal of variation in the history and management of congregational
endowments.

More striking, however, is the absence of theological considerations in
congregational leaders' approach to their endowments. The people who
talked to us about endowments were very articulate in speaking about the
funds, the management, and the priority systems, but there was a lack of any
theological language or ideas in the mix. Participants did not use biblical or
theological ideas or language other than "stewardship" and "mission." Instead, the operative language was of "responsibility," "accountability," and

"careful management." The guiding principle of handling endowments seemed to be what the courts describe as the "prudent man" rule.

Moreover, in talking about their congregation's endowment, people in these meetings tended to make references to experiences gathered from being on the boards of nonprofit organizations such as colleges, museums, private schools, and the like. The church leaders we talked with serve on many community boards, and they naturally draw on that experience in thinking about and managing their church's resources. As valuable as this experience is, it apparently contributes to a larger phenomenon in which it seems that the "religious" dimension of the congregation is one thing and the "financial" dimension quite another, not unlike Conway's findings with respect to clergy (Chapter 11 of this volume) or Wuthnow's findings with respect to individuals in general (Chapter 8 of this volume).

The low salience of theological concerns when it comes to managing congregational endowments also emerges in our survey data. We asked the congregational leaders who filled out our survey in each congregation to indicate whether they have high, medium, or low interest in exploration or discussion of a set of issues. Discussing "ethical and theological issues related to endowments" ranked ninth out of the 12 listed topics in level of interest expressed. Less interest—sometimes considerably less interest—was displayed for discussing ethical or theological issues than for developing a planned giving program, communicating with the congregation about the endowment, fund-raising, developing written policies, or managing the relationship with an investment manager. Overall, a "secular versus spiritual" split was evident both in the survey data and in our focus group conversations.

PRACTICAL CONCLUSIONS

This study of endowed Presbyterian churches is the first of its kind. It partakes of a broader trend by which Presbyterian churches gradually have moved from a policy of secrecy and guardedness about endowments to a policy of open communication. This study was exploratory in that it was meant to raise questions about how churches are similar and different from one another with regard to their endowments. Still, there are certain practical conclusions that emerge from this research. We highlight five.

1. Although invested funds are held by a relatively small percentage of all congregations, those congregations hold a vast amount of wealth. This

means that it is imperative for leaders in congregations with endowments to learn how to manage them responsibly and faithfully.

2. A striking finding in this study, as Ruger (1995) observed, is that *congregational spending rates are too high* if the objective is preserving the purchasing power of the endowments. Although a definitional ambiguity makes it difficult to determine the exact meaning of the observed rates at which congregations are spending from their endowments, it appears that the spending rates evident in our data will not preserve the purchasing power of these endowments.

3. Given the variation among congregations in the history and management arrangements of their endowments, it is unlikely that developing a single model policy or protocol for endowment management will be helpful. However, gathering and distributing the various written policies that congregations have developed to deal with their endowments might help congregational leaders to see the range of strategies and policies available to them.

4. These findings suggest that the higher the level of congregational dependency on its endowment, the more the endowment influences all aspects of church life, including a possible downward influence on annual giving. It seems, then, that a congregation's level of dependence on its endowment is a crucial variable for church leaders to monitor.

5. Perhaps the most burning practical question regarding endowments is their effect on member giving. Unfortunately, our data yield conflicting results on this matter. On the one hand, among churches with endowments, churches with larger endowments have *higher* annual giving per member. On the other hand, as mentioned in the previous paragraph, churches with higher levels of support from their endowment have *lower* average annual giving per member. Without additional, multivariate analysis that controls for such things as congregational size, the wealth of members, and other relevant factors, it is difficult to be sure what this pair of results means. On this important question, then, the jury still is out.

REFERENCES

Carr, Larry D. 1995. "Response." In *Survey of Endowed Presbyterian Churches* (no editor). Wilmington, DE: National Association of Endowed Presbyterian Churches.

Hoge, Dean R., and Loren Mead. 1995. "Survey of Endowed Presbyterian Churches." In *Survey of Endowed Presbyterian Churches* (no editor). Wilmington, DE: National Association of Endowed Presbyterian Churches.

Ruger, Anthony. 1995. "Policy Issues: Asset Allocation, Spending Rates, and Investing in the Future." In *Survey of Endowed Presbyterian Churches* (no editor). Wilmington, DE: National Association of Endowed Presbyterian Churches.

Chapter 11

Clergy as Reluctant Stewards of Congregational Resources

DANIEL CONWAY

This chapter continues the focus on the management of money already inside churches. In particular, it examines the extent to which church leaders—clergy—are equipped to develop and manage the human, physical, and financial resources that are needed to carry out their churches' mission. The questions addressed in this chapter include the following:

1. Do contemporary church leaders feel unprepared to deal with the multiplicity and diversity of pastoral and administrative duties that they are expected to carry out as leaders of their congregations?

2. Do clergy experience administrative functions as tedious or burdensome?

3. Do clergy feel that their seminary training prepared them well for their administrative and management responsibilities—especially those that involve raising and managing money?

AUTHOR'S NOTE: This chapter is adapted from the Introduction to *The Reluctant Steward: A Report and Commentary on The Stewardship and Development Study,* edited by Cecelia Hart Price. © 1992, Christian Theological Seminary and St. Meinrad Seminary, Indianapolis, IN; used with permission.

4. Do seminaries adequately prepare their students for administrative and financial leadership of congregations?

The data on which this chapter is based come from two 1991 surveys. A mailed survey of 136 accredited schools of theology in the United States and Canada provides information about programs and courses currently offered in the areas of leadership, management, and stewardship. This questionnaire was mailed to all 211 accredited schools of theology; 64 percent responded.

A telephone survey of a random sample of 200 Catholic and 200 Protestant pastors gauges clergy attitudes and perceptions about leadership, management, stewardship, and the kinds of programs pastors believe seminaries should offer to those who are preparing for ministry and to those who are already engaged in ministry. The clergy sample was selected from comprehensive lists in the National Catholic Directory and comparable directories published by the following Protestant denominations: United Methodist Church, Christian Church (Disciples of Christ), Evangelical Lutheran Church in America, Presbyterian Church (U.S.A.), United Church of Christ, Episcopal Church, and American Baptist Churches. Calls were made until the desired sample size of 200 Protestant and 200 Catholic clergy was obtained. Overall, 904 clergy were called to obtain our sample of 400, for a response rate of 44 percent.

The Catholic priests in our sample are (of course) all male, with a mean age of 55 years. On average, they had served as pastors for about 15 years, and they are evenly distributed among inner-city, urban, suburban, and rural parishes. The average size of the parishes they served is 1,100 families, with an average annual budget of approximately $400,000. The Protestant clergy in our sample are 90 percent male, with a mean age of 45 years. The average size of their congregations was less than 250 families, with an average annual budget of approximately $200,000.

FINDINGS

Clergy. Table 11.1 displays the percentage of pastors saying they are "extremely satisfied" or "very satisfied" with various aspects of their professional roles, skills, and training. (There are no significant differences between Protestant and Catholic clergy on any of these items, so the two samples are combined.) On the one hand, clergy are generally very satisfied with the theological and pastoral aspects of their role. More than 80 percent apparently take great satisfaction in their pastoral and theological duties, including

TABLE 11.1 Level of Clergy Satisfaction Regarding Duties, Skills, and Training

	Percentage Saying They Are Extremely or Very Satisfied With Duty, Skill, or Training
Duties:	
Pastoral	83
Theological	83
Administrative	28
Financial	33
Skills:	
Pastoral	87
Theological	80
Handling diversity	74
Personal leadership	72
Public relations	61
Handling social issues and problems	53
Financial management	51
Managing conflict	49
Personnel management	49
Managing own stress	46
Strategic planning	44
Seminary Training In:	
Theological and liturgical issues	77
Pastoral duties	51
Administrative duties	12
Financial duties	7

celebrating the liturgy, preaching the Word of God, helping and caring for people, and encouraging fellowship and social consciousness. On the other hand, far fewer clergy find substantial satisfaction in their administrative and financial duties. Indeed, of the pastors surveyed, only about one in three found either administrative or financial duties to be very satisfying. This striking absence of enthusiasm for administrative and financial duties is clearly evident, and to a nearly identical extent, among both Protestant and Catholic clergy.

A similar pattern emerged when pastors were asked to assess their skill at performing different aspects of their jobs. Clergy appear to be especially satisfied with their leadership skills within areas of theological or pastoral responsibility. Although over 60 percent of clergy are extremely or very satisfied with their religious and leadership skills, only about half the clergy in this sample were that satisfied with their ability and skills in administrative, financial, personnel, and strategic planning skills. Clergy apparently are less satisfied both with the administrative and financial aspects of their jobs and with their skill at executing these aspects of their jobs.

Pastors attribute their areas of strength and weakness to what they learned in the seminary. A small majority of those interviewed said they were extremely or very satisfied with their training in pastoral duties, and the vast majority were at least very satisfied with their training in theological and liturgical issues. By contrast, fewer than 15 percent of the pastors surveyed were very or extremely satisfied with the administrative and financial training they received.

Two other areas were explored in this survey: clergy attitudes about stewardship, and their experience and interest in continuing education in financial or management issues. Regarding stewardship attitudes, the results of this survey are consistent with other research that finds substantial differences between Protestant and Catholic clergy in the meaning they place on the concept of "stewardship." Catholic pastors tended to endorse a concept of stewardship that emphasized sharing with others the gifts that God has given to each individual and to the community. Protestant pastors tended to describe stewardship as managing well the gifts of time, talent, and treasure that individuals and communities have received from God.

When asked about their own efforts at continuing education, the pastors interviewed said that they try to take time for ongoing education in these areas. Most have taken five or six courses or workshops during their pastorates. These courses were most likely in the areas of strategic planning, personal time management, change in the modern congregation, and fund-raising. However, most had not participated in continuing education courses specifically dealing with the management of resources already in the parish. When asked directly about their interest in attending financial- or management-related short courses, clergy were not enthusiastic. As shown in Table 11.2, there was no suggested course topic in which more than 50 percent of either Protestant or Catholic clergy were very or extremely interested, and financial topics elicited the lowest levels of interest. Somewhat paradoxically, at the same time clergy express dissatisfaction with their seminary training in administrative and financial matters, they appear uninterested in continuing education courses or workshops that might help them to be better stewards of their congregations' human, physical, and financial resources.

The pastors survey shows, in sum, that many pastors neither like nor feel skilled at handling the administrative and financial aspects of their jobs. It

TABLE 11.2 Level of Clergy Interest in Courses on Various Subjects

	Percentage Saying They Are Extremely or Very Interested in Courses on Each Subject	
Subject	Protestants	Catholics
Strategic planning and leadership training	46	32
Change in the modern congregation	40	29
Human resource development	37	39
Communications or public relations	34	41
Congregation operations management	33	33
Personal time management	31	25
Theology of Christian stewardship	26	29
Personal stewardship of the minister	24	24
The meaning of money	23	17
Fund-raising, planning, and execution	20	18
Financial resource management	15	14
Economics or economic theory	14	12

NOTE: Only the first two Protestant/Catholic differences are statistically significant at the .05 level.

may not be an overstatement to say that these data seem to reveal a wish on the part of clergy to be left alone to exercise their theological, liturgical, and pastoral duties without the intrusion of irritating management and money matters. These matters, clergy in this sample seem to say, should be handled by someone else. Many pastors are, at best, only reluctant stewards of the church's material resources.

Theological Schools. Two out of every three accredited schools of theology in the United States and Canada responded to this survey, with many schools providing detailed catalogs of courses. The specific focus of this survey was to identify the extent to which seminaries offered courses in the areas of leadership, stewardship, and management. Courses in leadership were defined to include courses in pastoral and administrative decision making, consensus building, long-range planning, direction setting, financial management for complex institutions, institutional advancement, working with volunteers, and so on. Courses in stewardship included any offerings focused on the theology and practice of Christian stewardship—either the personal stewardship of individuals or the stewardship of organizations. Courses in management included personnel administration, time management, fund-raising, budgeting, facilities management, and the like. As Table 11.3 shows,

TABLE 11.3   Course Offerings in Protestant and Catholic Seminaries

Subject Area	Percentage Offering Courses in Each Area	
	Protestants	*Catholics*
Leadership	99	68
Stewardship	68	29
Management	80	55
All three areas	61	23

NOTE: Based on responses from 31 Catholic seminaries and 105 Protestant seminaries. All four differences between Protestant and Catholic seminaries are statistically significant at least at the .05 level.

most seminaries offer courses or workshops in these areas. Unlike among clergy, however, there are significant differences between Protestant and Catholic seminaries when it comes to course offerings. Protestant schools are substantially more likely than Catholic schools to offer leadership, steward-ship, or management courses.

Using the seminary catalogs to look more closely at course content, it was found that offered courses are much more likely to cover strategic management, leadership, and personnel issues than they are to deal specifically with monetary issues such as fund-raising, the meaning of money, or economics. In fact, seminary leaders are not uniformly supportive of the idea that seminaries *should* teach church leaders about the leadership, stewardship, and management of the church's resources. A portion of the seminary questionnaire tapping the opinions of either the school's dean or president asked whether the respondent agreed or disagreed with the statement, "The seminary has a distinct responsibility to teach its ministers the details of managing the local parish/congregation." Although the leaders of Catholic and Protestant seminaries tend to agree that good stewardship is essential to the pastor's calling, and that managing money has spiritual significance, only about 60 percent of Protestant seminary leaders and 25 percent of Catholic seminary leaders either "strongly" or "mostly" agree with this statement. As above, there is a large difference between Protestants and Catholics on this item.

PRACTICAL CONCLUSIONS

Today's pastors are, at best, reluctant stewards of their churches' human, physical, and financial resources. Although their hearts are in the right place, pastors, by their own admission, frequently lack the knowledge and experience that is required to oversee the development and management of resources (people, buildings, and money) that are needed to support the mission of the church. Furthermore, the training that church leaders receive in the areas of leadership, stewardship, and management tends to reinforce the strict separation between, on the one hand, the spiritual, theological, and pastoral dimensions of church leadership and, on the other hand, the material, administrative, and financial dimensions.

Two practical conclusions emerge from this work.

1. Seminaries probably can do more to train prospective clergy for the administrative and practical aspects of their work. The limited training opportunities that are currently available to future church leaders in the stewardship of human, physical, and financial resources normally are not a required part of the seminary curriculum; they are not, in general, regarded as an integral part of the theological and pastoral education that church leaders receive in the seminary. As a result, future church leaders do not receive systematic, integrated preparation for the management dimensions of pastoral ministry. Perhaps management courses could be required rather than elective for those going into the parish ministry. It is not clear, however, that seminary leaders are prepared to move in this direction.

2. Regarding continuing education for practicing ministers, it appears that clergy would not be keen to participate in workshops or courses on administrative matters even if seminaries, denominations, or other organizations offered such opportunities. This suggests that merely offering courses will not address the administrative skill deficit that apparently exists among clergy. The challenge, then, is to find ways to transmit needed skills to clergy who may be reluctant to seek them. How to do this is far from clear.

REFERENCE

Conway, Daniel. 1992. "Introduction." Pp. 5-27 in *The Reluctant Steward: A Report and Commentary on The Stewardship and Development Study*, edited by Cecelia Hart Price. Indianapolis: Christian Theological Seminary, and St. Meinrad, IN: St. Meinrad Seminary.

PART **III**

RELIGIOUS
ORGANIZATIONS
AND RESOURCES

Chapter 12

Financing Catholic
Elementary Schools

JOSEPH CLAUDE HARRIS

Contemporary Catholic elementary schools present us with something of a paradox. On the one hand, these schools have a reputation for high educational standards and for success in urban areas where public schools often are failing. At the same time, parochial schools have come under increased financial scrutiny and in several areas have closed for lack of funds. There has been increasing concern that parochial education has become too costly for parishes to maintain and too expensive for parents to afford.

The truth of the matter is that, over the past three decades, the financial situation of Catholic education has undergone a revolution. The changes, however, are not just in the total dollar amounts available to Catholic schools. There also have been significant changes both in the structure of the revenue streams—where the money comes from—and in the nature of ex-

AUTHOR'S NOTE: This chapter is adapted from *The Cost of Catholic Parishes and Schools,* by Joseph Claude Harris. © 1996, Sheed and Ward, Kansas City, MO; used with permission. The data in this chapter come mainly from published reports of the National Catholic Educational Association (NCEA), which has sponsored studies of Catholic schools since 1969. I will focus on changes since 1980.

penditures. This chapter describes the most important features of this change, focusing first on increasing costs and then on changes in revenue streams. As we'll see, these changes raise questions not just about financial viability but also about the very nature and mission of Catholic schools in American society.

WHAT HAPPENED TO
ELEMENTARY SCHOOL COSTS?

Costs have increased. The average Catholic elementary school required $184,372 to operate in 1980; in 1993 it cost $547,838, an increase of $363,466. The major factors producing this increase are inflation; increases in the cost of energy, insurance, and pensions; and a redesign of the elementary school program. In this section I parse out the inflation effect, leaving us with an estimate of the real cost increase, some of which is associated with new staffing and programming patterns.

Any analysis of the impact of inflation entails a discussion of the notions of current and constant dollars. Current dollars are simple: You need only sum the costs for a given period, and the total expenses represent current dollar cost for that period. Constant dollar accounting takes inflation into account. Making this adjustment backward in time—expressing 1980 costs in terms of 1993 dollars—the constant dollar cost for the average Catholic elementary school in 1980 was $323,321. The real cost increase in operating a Catholic elementary school, then, was $224,517. This means that 38 percent of the overall expenditure increase between 1980 and 1993 is attributable to inflation; 62 percent represents real cost increase.

What is behind this increase of $224,500 in real costs? Some of it comes from unavoidable increase in the price of energy, insurance, and pension. Importantly, though, it seems clear that at least some of this cost increase comes from investing in and improving the educational programming in Catholic elementary schools. The elementary school scene is no longer a situation where one classroom teacher instructs a class in all subjects in the same classroom. Not too many years ago, eight teachers, a principal, and a secretary staffed many schools. That this situation has changed is evidenced by the fact that total staff size in Catholic elementary schools increased from 96,739 in 1980-1981 to 112,199 in 1993-1994. Enrollment decreased during this period, which means that the pupil-staff ratio decreased from 23.56 in the early 1980s to 17.75 in the mid-1990s.

Substantively, this change reflects the fact that one teacher no longer teaches all subjects in one room. In addition, the number of courses has multiplied. Now classes in computers and music are virtually mandatory, the librarian is at least a part-time position, and so on. In short, Catholic schools have developed a broadened curriculum in pursuit of quality education, and some portion of the $224,500 real cost increase has gone toward purchasing this new programming.

PAYING THE BILLS

This section describes changes in the three basic funding streams for Catholic elementary schools: parish subsidies, tuition, and other funding.

At one time, parishes essentially paid for schools. On a personal note, I remember an $8 annual book charge as the only user fee required of the more than 600 students in our parish school in 1953. In those days, the pastor annually summarized parish and school efforts in one simple financial report because the parish program included a school. More generally, in 1969 the NCEA reported that parish subsidy represented 63 percent of program revenue for Catholic elementary schools. By 1980, parish subsidy funded 49 percent of the school budget, and this declined farther to 33 percent by 1993. It is interesting to note that parish support of schools varies considerably across regions. In the New England, Southeast, Mountain, and Far West regions, parishes give, on average, about 20 percent of their own income to their schools. In the Mideast, Great Lakes, and Plains regions, parishes give, on average, double that amount: 42 percent of parish revenue in these regions goes to schools.

It also is important to highlight the fact that the overall decline in the percentage of school budgets coming from the parish does *not* represent an absolute decline in parish contributions to schools. In constant 1993 dollars, the average parish subsidy to its school increased from $158,226 in 1980 to $180,863 in 1993. This point is worth emphasizing. Parish contributions to schools have in fact *increased* at a rate that slightly outpaces inflation. The decline in the proportion of school income that comes from the parish is produced by the fact that increases in parish subsidies have not kept pace with increases in costs, forcing schools to increase their dependence on other sources of income.

"Other funding" for Catholic elementary schools mainly means school-sponsored fund-raising, including auctions, jog-a-thons, candy sales, and the like. Catholic educational leaders have attempted over the years to expand efforts in this arena. For example, much of the fall 1994 issue of *Momentum*, a publication of the NCEA, was devoted to the topic of developing alternative sources of financing for Catholic education, including articles on development programs and marketing strategies. Such income has increased proportionately in recent years—from 11 percent of the average school budget in 1980 to 15 percent in 1993—but it remains a narrow funding stream for Catholic elementary schools.

Perhaps the most important change in recent decades is in the relative importance of a third funding stream: tuition. Neither parish subsidies nor additional fund-raising efforts began to fill the cost increases Catholic elementary schools have experienced in recent decades. The only available alternative was to turn to parents for money. As a result, tuition changed from 27 percent of school funding in 1969 to 40 percent in 1980 to 51 percent by 1993. From a family's perspective, the cost of sending children to a Catholic school has increased by 50 percent in terms of the proportion of household income it requires, from 2.3 percent of household income in 1980 to 3.6 percent in 1993 (see pages 78-80 in Harris [1996] for the details on this calculation).

Not surprisingly, regional variation in the extent to which schools depend on tuition income is the mirror image of the extent to which they depend on parish subsidies. In New England, the Southeast, the West, and the Far West, upward of 60 percent of the average school budget comes from tuition. In the Mideast, Plains, and Great Lakes states, tuition dependence ranges between one third and one half of an average school budget. In all regions, school dependence on tuition income has increased over this period.

If we assume that the bulk of the money categorized as "other funding" in fact comes from parents through means other than tuition, this means that the process of paying for Catholic elementary education has evolved from a 50-50 partnership between the parish and parents in 1980 to the 1993 situation where parents fund two thirds of the cost. The parish community has become a minority partner in the funding of elementary schools. In the meantime, Catholic schools are becoming less accessible because of increased tuition.

The accessibility of Catholic schools is further affected by the fact that there were 823 fewer of them in 1993 than there were in 1983. Bishops and pastors did not close these programs because they no longer saw a need or because somehow the programs failed. They closed for two main reasons. First, schools closed in cities when Catholics with children left urban neighborhoods to raise families in the suburbs. Second, programs shut down in rural areas where the average school budget grew dramatically while the resources of smaller rural parishes did not keep pace. Today, schools operate in about one third of parishes, a proportion very similar to the level that existed in 1884 (when 37 percent of parishes operated schools), and well below the 1960 level of 65 percent.

PRACTICAL CONCLUSIONS

This overview of the financing of Catholic elementary education suggests several practical conclusions. Let me highlight just four.

1. It is clear that the bulk of increased real costs in Catholic elementary education have been financed by sending larger tuition bills to parents. Continuing down this path means declining access to Catholic schools for students from lower-income families. Shifting onto another path means raising more money from parishes, from other sources, or both.

2. An earlier chapter observed that, per capita, Catholics give noticeably less than Protestants to their congregations. This suggests that it might be possible to raise parish income through stewardship programs or other means. Raising parish income could, in turn, translate into higher subsidies for schools.

3. The amount of funding from sources other than parishes or tuition remains very small. School administrators probably will not be able to change this very much without significant restructuring of public and private education financing of the sort envisioned by advocates of school voucher programs.

4. The overall trends in Catholic elementary school financing raise a larger question for school administrators and other Catholic religious leaders: How is the religious identity of a Catholic school to be maintained in the face of fiscal change that is making schools increasingly less dependent on parishes? From this perspective, discussing Catholic school finance leads to a larger discussion about the mission, goals, and identity of Catholic schools in the United States.

REFERENCE

Harris, Joseph Claude. 1996. *The Cost of Catholic Parishes and Schools.* Kansas City, MO: Sheed and Ward.

Chapter 13

Financing Protestant Theological Schools

ANTHONY RUGER

Theological schools have experienced substantial change in recent decades, change that influences funding streams in complex ways. One such change is demographic. Many institutions enrolled larger numbers of women, racial and ethnic minorities, and older or "second-career" students in the past two decades. The enrollment mix has further changed through the addition of Doctor of Ministry programs and off-campus "distance-learning" programs.

Changes in affiliated denominations also have affected schools. Broad social and historical changes have contributed to decreased denominational loyalties and church attendance in "mainline" religious traditions. As we shall see, changes in funding seem to reflect some of these trends. In addition, denominational conflicts—such as that experienced by the Southern Baptist Convention—have frequently focused on and affected a denomination's theological schools.

The national economy also has both hindered and helped theological schools over the past two decades. Inflation—arguably seminaries' single greatest economic enemy—reached an annual rate of more than 14 percent

AUTHOR'S NOTE: This chapter is adapted from *Lean Years, Fat Years: Changes in the Financial Support of Protestant Theological Education,* by Anthony Ruger. © 1994 by Auburn Theological Seminary, New York; used with permission.

in 1980 and subsided to less than 3 percent by 1991. Investment markets in the 1970s failed to beat inflation, yet rebounded strongly during the 1980s, even overcoming the effect of the October 1987 "crash." For seminaries, inflation and poor investment results made the 1970s economically grim and dismal; by contrast, the 1980s were almost entirely positive and salutary. Indeed, financial resources available to seminaries have, overall, shown increase in real terms since 1971. Theological schools increased their real (inflation-adjusted) revenue by about 10 percent between 1971 and 1981, and by about 45 percent between 1981 and 1991.

These increases notwithstanding, finances have remained a source of constant concern in theological education. In 1971, 46 percent of seminaries in the Association of Theological Schools (ATS) reported operating deficits ranging up to 20 percent of expenditures. That number was essentially unchanged in 1991, when at least 40 percent of theological schools showed operating deficits, with 10 percent showing deficits of more than 26 percent of revenues. Moreover, schools became increasingly aware during this period of the need to confront aging and deteriorating buildings and equipment. Little wonder, then, that seminaries developed sophisticated fund-raising operations and launched ambitious capital campaigns during the past two decades.

This chapter describes shifts in the revenue streams of Protestant theological schools. Most of the data focus on 67 schools in nine denominations for which data were systematically collected in 1971, 1981, and 1991. The nine denominations are the American Baptist Churches, the Christian Church (Disciples of Christ), the Episcopal Church, the Evangelical Lutheran Church in America (ELCA), the Lutheran Church-Missouri Synod, the Presbyterian Church (U.S.A.), the Southern Baptist Convention, the United Church of Christ, and the United Methodist Church. I use data from other sources to report trends since 1928, and I use data from a larger number of Protestant seminaries to report some contemporary differences among schools in these nine denominations; schools in other, smaller denominations; and inter- or nondenominational schools.

Over the long term, the revenue sources of theological education have changed markedly. Table 13.1 shows the main patterns: a decreasing dependence on endowed wealth and a growing reliance on student fees and gifts. While endowment revenue provided 61.1 percent of theological school revenues in 1928-1929, it provided only 30 percent in 1990-1991. Student fees, by contrast, rose from 11.4 percent of revenue in 1928-1929 to 22.5 percent in 1990-1991; gifts and grants rose from 14.6 percent to 41.7 percent of revenues over the same period. The rest of this chapter focuses on change in

TABLE 13.1   Changes in the Sources of Revenue for Protestant Theological
Schools

	Fiscal Year						
	1928/29	*1934/35*	*1954/55*	*1966/67*	*1970/71*	*1980/81*	*1990/91*
Percentage from each revenue source:							
Student fees	11.4	13.0	18.0	18.0	18.9	24.0	22.5
Endowment	61.1	54.0	32.0	31.3	22.6	24.5	30.0
Gifts and grants	14.6	24.0	35.6	42.3	52.1	43.9	41.7
Other	7.7	8.1	14.4	8.4	6.4	7.7	5.9

SOURCES OF DATA:
1928/29: May and Shuttleworth (1934:227).
1934/35 and 1954/55: Niebuhr, Williams, and Gustafson (1957:30).
1966/67: Arthur D. Little, Inc. (1968:38).
1970/71, 1980/81, and 1990/91: Financial data from 67 seminaries used throughout this chapter.

the 67 schools for which I have systematic data from 1971 to 1991. These
67 schools had $270,347,416 in revenue in 1990-1991.

STUDENT FEES

In the aggregate, student fee revenue is not and has never been the most
important source for theological schools. In strong contrast to colleges and universities, no denominational group in this study relies primarily
on student fees as a source of revenue. Put another way, theological schools
are not primarily tuition-driven.

It is important to note, however, that individual denominations vary
markedly in the extent to which their theological schools are dependent on
tuition. Of the nine denominations in this study, United Methodist schools
are most heavily dependent on tuition (35 percent of revenues); ELCA and
Presbyterian schools are the least dependent on tuition (each with 17 percent
of revenue from tuition). Schools in all nine denominations posted real (inflation-adjusted) increases in the absolute amounts of fees coming in over this
period.

The real increases in student fee revenue may be caused by increases in
the amount charged to each student, by increases in the number of students
enrolled, or by a combination of these two changes. I am not able to distinguish among these possible sources of change with the data at hand, but it is
relevant to note that theological school enrollment has shown considerable
growth since 1971. The total number of students enrolled in master's degree

programs in theological schools reporting to ATS rose from 29,885 in 1971 to 49,802 in 1991. The Doctor of Ministry degree enrollment increased tenfold, from 688 in 1971 to 6,944 in 1991. Some of this enrollment "growth" comes from increase in the number of schools reporting to ATS, but not all of it. I therefore speculate that enrollment increases have played a strong role in the absolute increase in revenue from tuition and fees. It is important to note, however, that increased master's level enrollment was almost completely produced by enrollment growth in master's programs *other than the Master of Divinity.* Masters of Divinity enrollment has been either stagnant or declining since the mid-1970s.

ENDOWMENT

Increasing real revenue from tuition has not made theological schools more tuition-dependent over this period, mainly because of the much larger growth in endowment income. On average, schools in these nine denominations receive 30 percent of their revenue from endowments, but this number varies widely among denominations. Missouri Synod Lutheran schools are least dependent on their endowments, relying on this source for only 8 percent of their revenues. Presbyterian, Disciples, and Episcopal schools, by contrast, all rely on endowment for more than 40 percent of educational and general revenue.

Schools in all nine denominations experienced real (inflation-adjusted) increase in endowment revenue between 1981 and 1991. Endowment revenue increased as a proportion of total revenue in seven of these nine. In the other two denominations (American Baptist Churches and United Church of Christ), endowment revenue declined slightly in relative importance because other types of revenue—tuition and gifts—increased more rapidly than endowment revenue during this period.

It also is relevant to note that the real growth of endowment revenue, while increasing for schools in all nine denominations, varied widely in the size of that increase, from as little as 10 percent for American Baptist schools to as much as 164 percent for Disciples schools. Why so much variance? First, schools have different investment strategies, constructing portfolios with different combinations of stocks and bonds. Second, some of the difference reflects the different amounts that schools were able to add to their endowments from gifts and bequests. Third, the amount of endowment revenue one has in the present reflects the school's past decisions to spend or reinvest endowment returns. Small changes in the amount of total return that is spent or reinvested can make a large difference over a long term.

GIFTS AND GRANTS

Overall, gifts and grants are the single largest source of revenue for theological schools throughout the period from 1971 to 1991. As with tuition, though, the huge increase in endowment revenue over this period means that gifts and grants have declined somewhat as a proportion of all revenue—from 52.1 percent in 1971 to 41.7 percent in 1991. As with the other revenue sources, each of the nine denominations showed real (inflation-adjusted) gains in the absolute amount of gifts and grants between 1981 and 1991.

Here, again, there is substantial variation among denominations. Presbyterian schools, on average, received only 24 percent of their 1991 revenue from gifts and grants. Schools affiliated with the Lutheran Church-Missouri Synod, the ELCA, and the Southern Baptist Convention, by contrast, all received at least 60 percent of their 1991 revenue from gifts and grants.

The real story about gifts and grants, however, concerns the shift away from denominational sources of support. For most denominations, the story is the same: Years ago, denominational support in the form of gifts from local churches, regional judicatories, and national church entities supplied most revenue. Over the years, though, church sources (as opposed to gifts from individuals, foundations, corporations, and fund-raising consortia) provided a smaller and smaller proportion of total gifts. Table 13.2 shows the trend for the nine denominations in this study. Two points are worth noting. First, today denominations vary widely in the proportion of their gifts from church sources. Only 30 percent of gifts and grants to United Church of Christ seminaries come from church sources, while 86 percent of gifts and grants to Southern Baptist schools come from church sources. Second, in all but one of these denominations, the proportion of gift and grant income from denominational sources declined, sometimes dramatically. The exception to this—the Episcopal Church—may reflect the growing success of a denominational funding plan initiated in the early 1980s that encouraged congregations to send "1 percent" contributions to Episcopal schools of their choosing.

Two factors, in varying degrees, can be said to have contributed to the evolution away from denominational funding to individual gifts. First, several denominations experienced financial strain at regional and national levels. Second, theological schools have become more intentional and skilled at

TABLE 13.2   Percentage of Gifts and Grants to Protestant Theological Schools
From Church Sources

	Year		
	1970/1971	*1980/1981*	*1990/1991*
Percentage from church sources in			
American Baptist Churches	41	45	32
Disciples of Christ	67	65	58
Episcopal Church	24	24	50
Evangical Lutheran Church in America	87	70	63
Lutheran Church-Missouri Synod	91	63	36
Presbyterian Church (U.S.A.)	76	57	35
Southern Baptist Convention	95	97	86
United Church of Christ	73	49	30
United Methodist Church	82	68	56

finding and developing a constituency of support among clergy and laity. This skill is evident when one looks at the sources for capital gifts—gifts for buildings and endowment. In aggregate, 80 percent of 1990-1991 capital gifts came from individuals. Fifteen percent of capital gifts came from foundations and corporations, some of which (in the case of family foundations and corporate matching gifts) were initiated by an individual. Local churches and regional and national campaigns provided comparatively little (5 percent) of the 1990-1991 capital contributions.

INTERDENOMINATIONAL SCHOOLS
AND SCHOOLS AFFILIATED WITH
OTHER DENOMINATIONS

Finally, I present data that contrast the revenue streams of the nine denominations at the center of this study with Protestant schools in other denominations and with interdenominational or nondenominational schools. These two categories are very diverse in character and heritage, although the "other denominations" tend to be much smaller than the nine focused on throughout this chapter. Table 13.3 presents the comparison.

Schools of smaller denominations collectively have few endowment resources and are therefore more dependent on gifts than schools in other categories. Inter- or nondenominational schools are more heavily dependent on student fees than other types. Interestingly, the gifts and grants revenue

TABLE 13.3   1991 Revenue Streams for Three Categories of Protestant
Denominations

	Nine Subject Denominations	Other Denominations	Inter/ Nondenominational Schools
Percentage of revenue from:			
Student fees	22	35	42
Endowment	30	8	21
Gifts and grants	42	51	26
Other	6	6	11
Percentage of gift and grant revenue from:			
Church sources	57	60	7
Individuals	26	29	75
Other	17	11	18

stream for smaller denominations is very similar to that of the nine large denominations in the extent of church support—60 percent versus 57 percent. Inter- or nondenominational schools, by contrast, receive very little support from churches or denominations. This last finding is not surprising, given the absence of denominational affiliation among these schools.

PRACTICAL CONCLUSIONS

The revenue trends reported in this chapter suggest some directions for policy. I will mention four.

1. Master of Divinity (M. Div.) enrollments are leveling off in North American theological education. The revenue implications of this stagnation or decline have been modest, however, because theological schools are not principally dependent on student fee revenues. Still, this situation has implications for the mission of theological schools. If a school finds itself working harder and harder to maintain a desired level of M. Div. enrollment and finds that the number of full-time students declines despite its best efforts, then it is time to consider the possibility that new programs or program forms might attract new constituencies. Continuing present programs in greatly reduced form may be another option. Either way, though, stagnating or declining M. Div. enrollments pose a fundamental question of mission for theologi-

cal schools: Whom will the institution seek to serve, and how will it seek to serve them?

2. Recent experience with endowments is instructive, since a decade of lean investment years was followed by a fat period of high returns. Schools must learn to manage their endowments wisely in both situations. One important principle is investment discipline. Trustees and administrators should have a well-thought-out approach to asset allocation, that is, to the decision to invest in different types of instruments. Disciplined investment also means persevering with a sound strategy and not overreacting to short-term, fear-inducing fluctuations in financial markets.

3. Another important endowment-related management principle is to balance present and future needs through a sound spending policy. Instead of simply spending all interest and dividends generated by the investments, trustees should adopt a policy of spending a specified and limited amount of the total return from investments. The unspent balance of the total return should be reinvested to protect the investment principal from erosion by inflation. The current norm in colleges and universities is a spending rate of 5 percent of a three-year average of the endowment market value.

4. Most theological schools find that current and capital gifts from individuals are growing faster than total gifts from church sources. One of the implications of this is that schools find themselves increasingly less dependent on denominations for fiscal support. While this may be welcome news for denominational budgets, it also means that the relationship between the school and the denomination may change. Such institutions may be seen less as subsidiaries of the denomination as their willingness to submit to denominational control can no longer be guaranteed by financial dependence. School and denominational leaders would be wise to consider the ecclesiological implications of this trend.

REFERENCES

Arthur D. Little, Inc. 1968. "Operation Income Components From 53 Accredited Seminaries." *Theological Education* 4(4), Supplement 2 (Summer):38.

May, Mark A., and Frank K. Shuttleworth. 1934. *Appendices,* Vol. 4 in *The Education of American Ministers.* New York: Institute of Social and Religious Research.

Niebuhr, H. Richard, Daniel Day Williams, and James M. Gustafston. 1957. *The Advancement of Theological Education.* New York: Harper & Brothers.

Ruger, Anthony. 1994. *Lean Years, Fat Years: Changes in the Financial Support of Protestant Theological Education.* New York: Auburn Theological Seminary.

Chapter **14**

Financing Parachurch Organizations

SHARON L. MILLER

Parachurch organizations have been an integral part of the American religious scene for well over a century, and they have grown rapidly in number since World War II. Foreign mission boards and church-sponsored colleges and seminaries are among the oldest and perhaps the most well known of these organizations, but they are joined today by a plethora of others: camps and conference centers, broadcast companies, rescue missions, relief and development organizations, evangelistic organizations, and social service organizations. Little research is available on these diverse organizations, and even less is known about their financial status, although all of them are vying for financial support.

To begin gathering information on these organizations, eight types of religious organizations were surveyed in 1994: foreign mission agencies, social service ministries, camps and conferences, rescue missions, denominational headquarters, schools, broadcast companies, and outreach ministries. Among other things, these surveys sought to learn the major sources of revenue for these parachurch institutions, how they solicit this revenue, and how the leaders of these organizations think about their financial situation. This project was coordinated by Wesley Willmer, Vice President of University Advancement at Biola University. This chapter presents an overview of findings from these eight surveys. Those interested in more detail should consult one or more of the specific reports on which this chapter is based.

Readers should note two aspects of these eight surveys. First, each of the eight organizational samples suffers from very low response rates (an average of 17 percent across all eight samples). Second, the lists of organizations from which most of these samples were drawn were overwhelmingly evangelical; in several, the sampling frame was exclusively evangelical. Readers should keep in mind both the low response rate and the evangelical bias in the samples when interpreting the findings from these surveys.

FOREIGN MISSIONS[1]

There are approximately 750 Protestant mission agencies in North America, with a total staff of 70,000 and annual expenditures of nearly $2 billion. A sample of 405 mission agencies was selected for this study, drawing largely from the evangelical tradition. A total of 98 usable questionnaires (24 percent) were returned.

The primary funding source for mission agencies is missionaries themselves. About two thirds of the agencies responding to this survey require their missionaries to raise the entire sum of their personal support. The agencies then support themselves by taking a portion—often 10 percent—of the missionary support dollars as administrative overhead. In each of the mission agencies responding to the survey, the primary source of income is individual and church giving to missionaries. Almost a quarter of mission agencies have endowments, but often such funds are not available for day-to-day operations.

Mission revenue in general is stagnant or declining. Many overseas mission agencies have plateaued in growth, and some are finding it increasingly difficult to maintain financial resources and personnel. Although a third of the agencies responding to this survey said that they expected growth and expansion in the next decade, fund-raising remains a real problem. Two thirds of the agencies said that older donors were not being replaced by younger donors, and the same proportion said that they are finding it increasingly difficult even to "get in the front door of churches." Over half stated that missionaries are taking longer to raise needed financial support, and 44 percent said that missionaries are increasingly dependent on fewer donors. A substantial minority of these agencies (22 percent) report running a deficit

1   This section is based on Engel (1996).

in 1992-1993, and 27 percent felt that their greatest income need was in meeting the annual budget. On average, only 29 percent of the names on these organizations' mailing lists are active donors.

SOCIAL SERVICE MINISTRIES[2]

This sample came from lists provided by the National Association of Evangelicals, CareNet, World Book of Churches, and the Evangelical Council for Financial Accountability. A total of 876 questionnaires were sent out, and 158 responses (18 percent) were received. The evangelical bias in this sample is particularly pronounced, and over half the responding agencies were involved in crisis pregnancy counseling.

Most of the executive directors of these organizations have had a relatively short tenure in their current position, and very few had any fund-raising experience prior to holding this position. Mailing lists of donors are small, and acquisition efforts are disappointing. Few major gifts have ever been received, little is done with planned giving, and most board members have little involvement in fund-raising.

Based on median statistics from the survey, the average mailing list consists of 1,490 individuals. A good proportion (56 percent) of these, however, are lapsed or nondonors, and less than 1 percent have given $1,000 or more within the past 12 months. The median number of churches, as opposed to individuals, on the mailing list was 56.

Over a third (39 percent) of these agencies are very dissatisfied with their fund-raising efforts. Only 25 percent of the organizations make an active effort to attract major donors, only 23 percent seek planned or deferred gifts, and only 5 percent had surveyed their constituency within the past three years to determine who gives and why. Nineteen percent reported that church presentations were the best method of new donor acquisition, while almost half felt that special events (dinners, auctions, etc.) worked best in this regard. Personal contact worked best for another 20 percent.

Half of the service agencies indicated that they intend to apply for foundation grants; one quarter intend to apply for corporation gifts. One third of the executives responding, however, say they do not have the time to prepare proposals, 24 percent say that their organization has limited appeal to foundations and corporations, and 22 percent feel that they lack the personnel or expertise to write grant proposals.

---

2   This section is based on Robertson (1996).

CAMP AND CONFERENCE MINISTRIES[3]

A total of 340 Christian camps and conference centers from 45 states returned their surveys—23 percent of the 1,500 that were mailed out. The camps that responded ranged in size from a low of 40 people to a high of 70,000 people served in 1993. The median camp in the study had 150 beds and served about 3,000 persons annually. Half of the camps were owned by a denomination or a group of churches within a single denomination; 27 percent were owned by independent, nonprofit, parachurch organizations or ministries.

The vast majority of camp operating funds—an average of 83 percent—comes from fees, the remaining 17 percent from donations. Smaller camps and conference centers were more dependent on donations than were camps with higher budgets. These donations came from a variety of sources. Fifty percent raised income from churches; 32 percent of the camps indicated that they raised income from denominational sources; 15 percent had capital fund drives. The financial well-being of most of these centers seems to be secure—70 percent indicated no long-term debt—and those that were in long-term debt were usually paying for land or facilities.

Despite the financial health of these centers, many of the camp or conference executives expressed frustration with fund-raising. Forty-one percent of the surveyed directors indicated that their fund-raising skills were "below average" or "weak." Almost half (46 percent) felt like they were "begging" when they did fund-raising, and one third were afraid to talk with wealthy people. Over 60 percent of directors expressed dissatisfaction with their board's involvement in soliciting donors or in referring donor prospects.

RESCUE MISSIONS[4]

The International Union of Gospel Missions (IUGM) estimates that there are at least 500 rescue missions—organizations that provide shelter and food for the homeless and destitute—in the United States, about half of which are members of IUGM. This organizational population was surveyed twice in recent years—in 1994, along with the other surveys described in this chapter, and also in 1993, in a Pepperdine University survey. In both surveys the samples were drawn from the membership lists of IUGM and the National

---

3   This section is based on Kluth (1996).
4   This section is based on Fahs (1996).

Association of Evangelicals. Given this sampling frame, it is not surprising that virtually all (99 percent) of the 70 responding missions say that they have a spiritual emphasis to their ministry. Almost all provide meals (or vouchers for off-site meals), clothing, and shelter. Sixty-two percent provide some form of education, either for the children of the homeless or literacy and job training for adults. Many provide psychological counseling, medical care, and recreation, and several target specific groups such as battered women and their children, runaway youth, or the mentally disabled.

Ninety-four percent of the executive officers of these organizations are male. The average executive spends 40 percent of his time in fund-raising and development activities, and over two thirds of the directors said that they planned to increase their development staff in the next year or two. Three quarters of the directors said that they had attended a fund-raising conference or seminar at some point in their career. Forty-seven percent rated their development skills as strong or above average, another 37 percent said they were average, while only 15 percent said their skills were weak or below average.

Despite their skills, the directors face frustrations and disappointments. Thirty-eight percent said they were somewhat or very dissatisfied with their ability to attract major donors, 45 percent were somewhat or very dissatisfied with the planned giving initiatives of their mission, and 30 percent were concerned that their donor base was shifting. Over one third (35 percent) said that donor attrition was a rising problem.

Most of the missions are highly dependent on financial contributions from individuals, and more than 90 percent use newsletters and direct mail to communicate with and solicit potential donors. The median mailing list has 9,465 units, 200 of which are churches or religious groups, 40 of which are government bodies, and 101 of which are corporations. Many of the names on the list, however, are nonproductive. On average, 42 percent of the names either have never given or have given nothing in the previous 12 months. Most (81 percent) of these organizations have not surveyed their constituency in the past three years to determine who gives and why.

Experience with different fund-raising methods seems to be mixed. While 40 percent of directors said that direct mail worked best in acquiring new donors, another 24 percent were disappointed with the results of direct mail. Newspaper ads proved to be a good tool for 22 percent of those seeking new donors, but they proved to be a disappointment for 17 percent of the others. Foundations were another source of funding, and the median organization submitted six proposals in the previous year. The grants received appear to be small, however, with the median being $9,950.

RELIGIOUS BODY HEADQUARTERS[5]

▓ This survey was sent to 220 denominations listed in the *Yearbook of American and Canadian Churches,* but only 31 denominations (14 percent) returned completed questionnaires. Still, these 31 respondents represent about a third of all Protestant congregations in the United States.

A quarter of the denominations surveyed said that most denominational funds came from congregational assessments, often figured on a per member basis. Fifty-six percent said that support of the denominational headquarters was voluntary. Almost two thirds of the respondents said that they thought local churches were raising more money than before but forwarding less to the denominational headquarters, corroborating results obtained from other sources (see Chapter 2 in this volume).

When denominations were asked if they had developed specific strategies for reaching and educating younger donors, 29 of the 31 responding denominations said "no." When asked if they had made any efforts to find new donors, 61 percent said "no." Eighty-five percent of denominations say that they rely primarily on local pastors for communicating financial needs to the people, and these pastors are contacted an average of five times a year about the financial needs of the denomination. Forty percent of the responding denominations, however, report that pastors are passive or even hostile concerning the financial needs of the denomination.

How are denominations attempting to deal with their financial crisis? Seventy percent of those reporting say that they have cut their budgets through program reductions, 48 percent have drawn on reserve finances, 43 percent have sent out emergency appeals to raise money, and two thirds have cut staff in the past decade. Only 38 percent of responding denominations report that they have a written fund-raising strategy.

SCHOOLS[6]

▓ To assess the health and financial status of religious schools, surveys were mailed to 3,208 schools, many of them members of two different associations of Christian schools. Almost 19 percent were returned. Roman Catholic schools were not included in this sample.

---

5   This section is based on Schmidt (1996).
6   This section is based on Lockerbie (1996).

The smallest school in the sample had four students, the largest had 2,167. Almost two thirds of the schools (65 percent) reported an increase in enrollment in the previous year; 13 percent reported a decrease. Fifty-seven percent of the schools were owned or operated by a single sponsoring church, and 23 percent were owned or operated by parents. Even in those schools owned by an individual church, 78 percent of the students were not a part of the sponsoring church.

In a pattern similar to that of contemporary Catholic primary schools (see Chapter 12 of this volume), the majority of funds for schools in this sample come from tuition payments, with the average school receiving $277,000 in tuition payments and $46,000 from other sources. With the average school in this sample enrolling 170 students, this amounts to $1,900 expended on each pupil. While elite independent schools may spend as much as $14,500 per pupil, the national average for public schools is $5,100.

In a typical school, additional funds come from a wide variety of sources: the sponsoring church, board members, parents, other friends of the school, alumni, corporations, and product sales. The typical school mailing list contains a median of 400 names. Most of the people on the mailing list, however, are nondonors. Only 7 percent of the schools had surveyed their constituency within the last three years to determine who gives and why they give; only one quarter (23 percent) have a planned or deferred giving program.

Although only a minority of students in these schools (an average of 22 percent) come from the sponsoring church, most schools (70 percent) received no financial support from other churches in the area. Forty-three percent of the schools indicate that they will be targeting churches in their future fund-raising efforts. Schools had submitted a median number of two proposals to foundations in the previous year, but 69 percent said that they had never received a grant from a foundation.

Only 14 percent of surveyed schools said that they were very or somewhat satisfied with their ability to attract new donors. Over a third (35 percent) said they were disappointed with the results of direct mail appeals, and 42 percent were disappointed with fund-raising events (e.g., banquets) they had sponsored. Few school administrators (17 percent) had used outside consultants within the last year to help in developing gift support, and only 20 percent said that they were going to use outside expertise in the coming year. Only 29 percent of those responsible for raising funds had ever attended any conference or seminar on fund-raising.

BROADCAST COMPANIES[7]

By 1996 there were more than 1,300 radio stations with Christian formats in the United States. Since the late 1960s, Christian television programs and even networks have entered the market. Surveys were sent to 909 radio and television stations and program producers on the mailing list of the National Religious Broadcasters. A total of 112 (12 percent) responded. Of those responding, 56 percent identified themselves as radio stations, 10 percent as television stations, 34 percent as radio program producers, and 17 percent as television producers.

These stations and producers report a median annual income of $204,700 and a mean of $706,900. Their undesignated funds come primarily from direct mail campaigns (a median of $155,400) and the sale of commercial time (a median of $51,900). Lesser amounts come from corporate giving (a median of $24,500) and foundations (a median of $12,000). Additional income comes from the sale of books, tapes, and other material, and 30 percent report that they are raising more revenue this way.

Because direct mail is one of the primary sources of income, the size of the station's or producer's mailing list becomes an indication of its fund-raising potential, and growth or decline in that mailing list is an indication of future support. Radio stations in this sample reported virtually no growth in their mailing lists from 1991 to 1993, and television stations and programmers reported a 10 percent to 20 percent decline in the number of active donors on their mailing lists. Telethons are used by 42 percent of the respondents, and two thirds report that they solicit funds on the air. Only 21 percent have used outside consultants to help in developing gift support.

In most, perhaps all, donor pools, the majority of the money comes from a relatively small proportion of the givers (see Chapter 4 of this volume for an explanation of this phenomenon). Religious broadcast companies are not an exception to this general pattern. At the same time, only one quarter of the organizations specifically cultivated large donors (those giving $1,000 or more), and 44 percent expressed some dissatisfaction with their ability to solicit major donors. Most broadcast companies in this sample (74 percent) do not solicit planned gifts, although 42 percent of television stations said that they received funds through this method.

Only 25 percent of broadcasters have tried to solicit funds from foundations. When asked what were the biggest obstacles to finding foundation funding, 27 percent said they do not have a person on staff with the time/ex-

---

7   This section is based on Clark and Virts (1996).

pertise to write proposals; 24 percent said they were too busy with urgent needs to spend time on proposals; and 21 percent said they needed help knowing which foundations to ask for funds.

OUTREACH MINISTRIES[8]

The eighth survey focused on outreach ministries, defined as "Christian organization(s), working primarily in North America, and focusing on such ministry as evangelism, prisoner/ex-offender outreach, home missions, youth and campus ministries, and Bible and literature ministries" (McCabe and Campbell 1996:xi). What sets these particular types of organizations apart from others considered in this chapter is their specific focus on religious conversion.

A sample of these organizations was drawn from the Billy Graham Center on Prison Ministry and from the membership lists of the National Association of Evangelicals and the Christian Stewardship Association. Over 1,300 surveys were mailed; 116 (9 percent) were returned. Of those responding to the survey, 52 percent said that they were evangelism and discipleship ministries, 40 percent were prison/ex-offender outreach ministries, 25 percent were home missions organizations, and 24 percent did youth and campus outreach. These are small organizations, with a median number of eight full-time and three part-time employees. The mailing lists of these organizations had, on average, 3,500 names, of which about 14 percent were active donors. Only 18 percent of these organizations had surveyed their donors within the previous three years.

Respondents reported that personal visits were the most effective way to acquire new donors (mentioned by 26 percent), followed by church presentations (20 percent) and special events (16 percent). Direct mail was the least effective method in the eyes of these respondents. Most respondents (53 percent) were somewhat or very dissatisfied with board members' ability to refer donor prospects, and an even higher percentage (59 percent) were dissatisfied with the board's ability to solicit donors personally.

PRACTICAL CONCLUSIONS

These eight organizational populations are, obviously, very diverse. They vary, for example, in the extent to which they are primarily dependent on

---

8   This section is based on McCabe and Campbell (1996).

donations or fees, and they vary in their overall financial health. Still, several practical conclusions emerge from this work.

1. In each of these organizational populations, there is substantial diversity when it comes to organizational size. Moreover, size differences often appear related to financial characteristics, such as the existence of an endowment, relative dependence on donations, and the capacity to pursue foundation or corporate grants. It seems fair to conclude that, whatever the arena of activity, the financial challenges facing small parachurch organizations are likely to be fundamentally different from the challenges facing large organizations.

2. A striking finding from these studies is the rudimentary status of what we might call the fund-raising infrastructure of these organizations. Very few survey their donors, actively seek new donors, target major donors, develop planned giving programs, have professional development staff, or have boards actively involved in fund-raising. Consonant with the first point, all of this infrastructure is less likely to be present in smaller organizations. This suggests that there may be room for parachurch organizations, even small ones, to develop their capacity for seeking additional funds. Making better use of boards and board members is one obvious step that many organizations probably could take.

3. Most of these parachurch organizations (with the exception of foreign mission agencies and denominations) report only minimal connection with local churches. Most donation support comes directly from individuals, not from congregations. Developing stronger ties with congregations may be a wise strategy for parachurch organizations.

4. Similarly, these organizations report only very minimal efforts at submitting proposals to foundations or corporations. Developing skills in proposal writing, or working with people who have such skills, may be a worthwhile investment for leaders of parachurch organizations.

5. Finally, it seems that few of the executives in these organizations have developed an explicit theological basis for their fund-raising. Secular marketing and fund-raising practices (although rarely used) are looked to for answers to financial woes, and there is little evidence of attempts to assess critically the appropriateness of importing secular fund-raising models into religious organizations. The relative absence of theological reflection when it comes to financial and management issues is not unique to parachurch organizations—see Chapters 10 and 11 for other examples—but leaders of these organizations still may wish to find ways to encourage deeper theological reflection on financing parachurch organizations.

REFERENCES

Clark, David W., and Paul H. Virts. 1996. *Changing Channels: A Guide to Financing Christian Broadcast Ministries.* Milwaukee, WI: Christian Stewardship Association.

Engel, James F. 1996. *A Clouded Future? Advancing North American World Missions.* Milwaukee, WI: Christian Stewardship Association.

Fahs, Ivan. 1996. *From Soup and a Sermon to Mega-Mission: A Guide to Financing Rescue Missions.* Milwaukee, WI: Christian Stewardship Association.

Kluth, Brian. 1996. *Out of the Woods: A Guide to Funding Camp and Conference Ministries.* Milwaukee, WI: Christian Stewardship Association.

Lockerbie, D. Bruce. 1996. *From Candy Sales to Committed Donors: A Guide to Financing Christian Schools.* Milwaukee, WI: Christian Stewardship Association.

McCabe, Tom, with Bruce Campbell. 1996. *Inside Outreach: A Guide to Christian Outreach Ministries.* Milwaukee, WI: Christian Stewardship Association.

Robertson, Sara Anne. 1996. *Helping the Hurting: A Guide to Financing Christian Social Service Ministries.* Milwaukee, WI: Christian Stewardship Association.

Schmidt, J. David. 1996. *Choosing to Live: Financing the Future of Religious Body Headquarters.* Milwaukee, WI: Christian Stewardship Association.

Chapter 15

Religious Nonprofits in California

MICHAEL O'NEILL

Nonprofit organizations, many of them funded in part or in whole by religious bodies, play a vitally important role in the United States. These agencies provide health, education, artistic, religious, social, and other services to millions of Americans. They provide employment for eight million people, have annual revenues of $500 billion, and use the services of 80 million volunteers. This chapter provides an overview of religious nonprofit organizations in the state of California. It is based on a larger 1995 study of California's nonprofit sector. This larger study was intended to answer three basic questions about the state's nonprofit sector: How many nonprofit organizations are there in California? How many people do they employ? How much money do the state's nonprofits receive and spend annually?

To answer these questions, we drew on a wide variety of governmental and private data sources. Finding good data on nonprofit organizations is often a challenge. For example, agencies with less than $25,000 in annual revenue—nearly 80 percent of California's nonprofits—are not required to file reports with the IRS. Neither are California's 24,000 religious organizations. To fill this gap we drew on data from more than 20 major sources, including the U.S. Census of Service Industries, U.S. Census of Population and Housing, California Catholic Conference, and over 100 religious organizations that publish documents on employment and services. Overall, we

131

found 120,000 nonprofit organizations in California in 1995. These organizations employed 750,000 people and receive and spend $52 billion a year.

This chapter has two parts. First, I focus on the 24,000 religious organizations providing religious services in the state of California. These organizations are compared to the secular membership organizations and to the civilian labor force as a whole in terms of their employment patterns and expenditures. Second, I present data on the extent to which religious organizations are present in the social service, health, and education segments of the nonprofit sector. Readers interested in more detail should see the full report (*California Nonprofit Organizations* 1995) from which this chapter is adapted.

RELIGIOUS ORGANIZATIONS
PROVIDING RELIGIOUS SERVICES

The California Secretary of State lists approximately 24,000 organizations formed primarily for religious purposes. These organizations constitute about 20 percent of the state's nonprofit sector, employ about 10 percent of the state's nonprofit employees, and account for about 7 percent of the total amount of money received and spent by the sector.

Many of these organizations, of course, are traditional religious congregations. A 1990 county-by-county count of religious congregations found about 14,400 Judaeo-Christian congregations in California (Bradley et al. 1992). The large difference between this figure and the Secretary of State's figure may be explained by three factors. First, religious organizations that are not churches or other places of worship were counted by the Secretary of State but not by the 1990 study. Second, congregations that are other than Jewish or Christian were excluded from the 1990 study. Third, and perhaps most important, the 1990 study counted congregations only in 133 of the 246 denominations invited to participate in that study. Congregations that are independent of any denomination also were excluded from that count.

Whatever the actual number of congregations, it is clear that, although the West has historically had a lower level of formal religious involvement than the Northeast, Southeast, and Midwest, California has a large and active religious sector, including every part of the religious spectrum: Catholic, Protestant, Jewish, Muslim, Buddhist, Scientologist, and New Age. While 77 percent of the state's adults identify themselves as Christian, Californians are nearly twice as likely as Americans generally to identify themselves as Jewish, Muslim, Buddhist, or other non-Christian faiths—6.0 percent versus 3.3 percent. Eighty-three percent of Californians identify themselves with some religion, as compared with 90 percent nationally (Kosmin and Lachman 1993).

Organizations formed primarily for religious purposes are somewhat unique among nonprofits. Unlike other nonprofits, they are not required to submit Form 990 and similar financial reports to the IRS and state government agencies. Also unlike many other nonprofits, congregations receive little money from foundations and corporations, government, endowments, or the sale of products and services. The bulk of religious congregation revenue comes from member donations.

Some statistical studies of nonprofit organizations have excluded organizations formed primarily for religious purposes on the grounds that these organizations are not required to file 990 reports and therefore are too difficult to study. However, there are many data sources, including some governmental sources, on these organizations. For instance, the California Employment Development Department collects data on religious organization employment. The state's Franchise Tax Board collects data on religious property tax exemption. The 1990 U.S. Census of Population and Housing asked about nonprofit versus for-profit or government employment, with religion as one of the employment categories. The 1989-1990 National Survey of Religious Identification (NSRI) was based on a representative sample of 113,000 Americans, including more than 10,000 Californians (Kosmin and Lachman 1993:2, 77). A 1990 national study included information, by county and by denomination, on the number of churches, members, and adherents in California (Bradley et al. 1992). The Gallup Organization conducts yearly surveys of religious activity. Independent Sector conducts a biennial survey of religious giving and volunteering. Many religious denominations collect data on their churches and members and make this information publicly available. Also, a large number of religious organizations—nearly half of those in California—file for tax exemption and, in some cases, file 990 reports even though they are not required to do so. In summary, presenting statistical data on the religious part of the nonprofit sector offers unique challenges but is by no means impossible.

A significant aspect of the financial situation of any nonprofit organization is its payroll. In this section, we are able to add to knowledge about the financing of American religion by focusing on some characteristics of employees of religious organizations. We are able to compare employees of organizations formed primarily for religious purposes with employees of other organizations, and we also are able to report two estimates of the aggregate amount spent by these organizations. The basic data regarding employees are presented in Table 15.1. This table compares employees of religious

TABLE 15.1   Three Types of Employees in California, 1990

	Civilian Labor Force	Nonreligious Membership Organizations	Religious Organizations
Number	12,391,058	44,937	75,672
Percentage male	54.7	43.2	53.2
Percentage under age 35	48.9	37.6	27.5
Percentage over age 50	16.9	27.1	35.6
Percentage non-Hispanic white	60.0	73.5	74.3
Percentage with BA degree or more	24.8	29.5	45.0
Percentage earning $35,000 or more	24.3	24.2	12.4

SOURCE: U.S. Department of Commerce, Bureau of the Census, *1990 Census of Population and Housing,* Public Use Microdata Sample (PUMS): 5-Percent Sample.

organizations with employees of secular membership organizations and with California's civilian labor force as a whole.

As noted earlier, California religious organizations employed about 76,000 people in 1990, constituting about 10 percent of nonprofit sector employees. There are several significant and interesting differences between religious and other nonprofit employees, and between religious workers and the labor force generally. Compared to the civilian labor force in general, religious employees are more likely to be white, older, better educated, and poorly paid. Compared to employees of secular nonprofit membership and labor organizations in California, they are more likely to be male, older, better educated, and, again, poorly paid.

According to the 1990 census, 53 percent of religious organization employees were male. This is similar to the percentage male in the civilian labor force as a whole, but substantially higher than in secular membership and labor organizations, where only 43 percent of employees were male in 1990. Also, nonprofit labor market studies have consistently found that only one third of nonprofit employees in general are male.

Religious workers were far more educated than other workers in the state: 45 percent of religious workers reported holding a bachelor's or higher degree, as compared with 25 percent of workers generally and 29.5 percent of workers in secular membership and labor organizations. Religious workers also were older than the general labor force: only 27.5 percent of religious workers were under 35 in 1990, compared with 49 percent of all workers and 38 percent of workers in secular membership and labor organizations. Looking at the flip side, almost 36 percent of religious workers were over 50 in 1990, compared with 17 percent in the civilian labor force as a whole and 27 percent in secular membership and labor organizations. Finally, 74 percent of religious workers were non-Hispanic white, compared to 60 percent of all workers.

Despite being older, better educated, more male, and more white—characteristics typically associated with higher incomes—religious workers are a strikingly low paid group. Only 12.4 percent of religious workers reported earning more than $35,000 a year in 1990, compared with 24 percent of workers both in secular membership and labor organizations and in the civilian labor force as a whole. These numbers may somewhat understate the compensation received by religious workers. Thirty-five percent of these workers are clergy, and many religious congregations supply housing, cars, and other benefits that may not appear in self-reported income statements. It is unlikely, however, that this factor would account for enough of the income difference to change the basic conclusion that employees of religious organizations are more poorly paid than employees in the rest of the labor force or in the rest of the nonprofit sector.

Because of an interpretation of the First Amendment to the U.S. Constitution, religious nonprofit organizations are not required to file yearly 990 reports with the IRS, as are other nonprofit agencies with gross revenue exceeding $25,000 a year, and religious organizations are typically exempted from other government data collection, such as the Census of Service Industries. This leaves a large financial information gap with respect to a significant part of the nonprofit sector.

Switching our attention to total expenditures, we used a variety of sources and several reasonable assumptions to estimate that California religious organizations—by which we mean here organizations formed primarily for religious purposes—spent $3.5 billion in 1993. Of this amount, 86 percent went for salaries, benefits, building and property costs, local congregation activities, and the like. The other 14 percent was spent on "benevolences," expenditures for the larger mission of the church, beyond local congregational needs. These include expenditures for international missions, national and local charities, denominational administration, seminaries, and the like.

This budget estimate may be too conservative. According to a 1990 national study of churches and church membership, California had 9.2 percent of the nation's Judaeo-Christian religious adherents (Bradley et al. 1992). Independent Sector estimated that in 1991 the total revenues of American religious congregations were $48.4 billion, and the total expenditures $47.6 billion (Hodgkinson and Weitzman 1992). If the Independent Sector figures are correct, and assuming that number of adherents is closely related to revenue and expenditures, California religious organization revenue and expense would be between $4 and $5 billion.

RELIGIOUS ORGANIZATIONS DELIVERING SOCIAL SERVICES, HEALTH, AND EDUCATION

Focusing on organizations formed primarily for religious purposes ignores, of course, the extent to which religious organizations are an important part of other arenas in the nonprofit sector. Religious organizations in fact cross nearly all nonprofit lines. In addition to local congregations, religious groups also operate schools and colleges, hospitals, social service agencies, and even some grantmaking, advocacy, and cultural groups. Indeed, some of the largest nonprofit organizations in California are religiously affiliated: in social services, World Vision, Hebrew Home for the Aged, YMCA, and Catholic Charities; in health care, Cedars-Sinai Medical Center, Mercy Healthcare, and Loma Linda University Medical Center; and in higher education, Santa Clara University, Loyola Marymount University, the University of San Francisco, and others. Religiously affiliated elementary and secondary schools account for 80 percent of the private K-12 enrollment and 7 percent of total K-12 enrollment. Fifty-nine percent of the enrollment in California's religious primary and secondary schools is in Roman Catholic schools. A useful next step in this research would be to compare the religious organizations in these sectors to secular organizations in terms of their revenue streams, performance, and other characteristics.

PRACTICAL CONCLUSIONS

This chapter has provided an overview of religious organizations in California's nonprofit sector. Two practical conclusions emerge from this overview.

1. The relatively low pay of employees in religious organizations, especially given those employees' higher than average level of education, is striking. Managing payroll is an important part of responsible stewardship in any nonprofit organization, and the salary comparisons described here ought to provoke discussion of compensation issues in religious nonprofit organizations. What do these comparisons suggest about how religious organizations

prioritize their spending relative to other nonprofits? What do they suggest about religious organizations' capacity to compete for the efforts of the most talented and skilled individuals?

2. Comprehending the financing of American religion means attending to more than the financing of congregations and organizations formed primarily for religious purposes. Religious organizations form a significant component of the social service, health, and education sectors in the nonprofit economy. Leaders concerned with the financial health of religious organizations, and leaders interested in the financial health of organizations in the nonprofit sector in general, would both benefit from increased knowledge about religious organizations that are formed for other than religious purposes.

REFERENCES

Bradley, Martin B., Norman M. Green, Jr., Dale E. Jones, Mac Lynn, and Lou McNeil. 1992. *Churches and Church Membership in the United States, 1990: An Enumeration by Region, State, and County Based on Data Reported for 133 Church Groupings.* Atlanta, GA: Glenmary Research Center.

California Nonprofit Organizations, 1995. 1995. San Francisco: University of San Francisco, Institute for Nonprofit Organization Management.

Census of Population and Housing, 1990: Public Use Microdata Samples U.S. 1992. Washington, DC: Bureau of the Census.

Hodgkinson, Virginia A., and Murray S. Weitzman. 1992. *From Belief to Commitment: The Community Service Activities and Finances of Religious Congregations in the United States, 1993 Edition.* Washington, DC: Independent Sector.

Kosmin, Barry A., and Seymour P. Lachman. 1993. *One Nation Under God: Religion in Contemporary American Society.* New York: Garland.

Chapter 16

Small Religious Nonprofits in Illinois

Kirsten A. Grønbjerg
Sheila Nelson

This chapter focuses on small religious nonprofit human service organizations (SRNPs).[1] Drawing on a 1991 survey of Illinois human service nonprofits, we compare the organizational and financial characteristics of SRNPs to secular nonprofits of similar size and type. We also compare small nonprofits—both religious and secular—to large nonprofits, allowing us to understand better which features of SRNPs are more related to their smallness and which are more related to their religiousness.

Many researchers focus primarily on IRS-registered, tax-exempt nonprofits because it is convenient to do so. Limiting the population of eligible organizations in this manner, however, provides too narrow a view of the nonprofit landscape and of SRNPs in particular. For our 1991 study of human service organizations in Illinois, the IRS list was supplemented with the current edition of the *Human Care Services Directory of Metropolitan Chicago* (1992). This added 1,075 organizations to the IRS list of charitable tax-exempt hu-

---

1 SRNPs are defined as organizations that (1) are affiliated with a religious tradition but are not themselves religious congregations, (2) engage in any of several human-service-related activities, and (3) have fewer than 20 full-time equivalent staff or annual expenditures under $500,000.

man service organizations, accounting for 26 percent of the total sampling frame. This chapter reports findings from the 398 organizations that provided information on both revenues and religious affiliation in response to our survey. Of these, 14 percent are SRNPs, 58 percent are small secular nonprofits, 6 percent are large religious nonprofits, and 22 percent are large secular nonprofits. Religious nonprofits thus comprise one fifth of this sample of human service organizations in Illinois.

There are good reasons to believe that these numbers substantially underestimate both the religious component of this organizational population and the SRNP component in particular. First, both small organizations and religious organizations are dramatically underrepresented in the IRS Business Master File (Grønbjerg 1994). Second, our sample was drawn from lists that included only separately incorporated organizations. This means that human service programs carried out in congregations but not separately incorporated do not appear in the sampling frame. We note with some distress, for example, that our sample included *no* child care centers or preschools affiliated with the Catholic Church. We suspect that this reflects the exclusion of Catholic-affiliated child care centers and preschools from the sampling frame and not just their nonresponse to the survey. Thus, the fact that SRNPs, even with all of the factors pushing them out of the sampling frame, still compose as much as 14 percent of the sample, suggests that, although largely invisible to researchers, they are sizable in number and significant in impact. At the same time, given the limitations of our data and the small number of SRNPs in our sample, our findings should be considered suggestive and should be interpreted with caution. Readers interested in more information about our sample, methods, and findings should see the article by Grønbjerg and Nelson (1998), from which this chapter is adapted.

FINDINGS

Table 16.1 summarizes our findings by highlighting comparisons among small and large nonprofits and among secular and religious nonprofits. We first describe several basic organizational features and then present data on financial characteristics.

Organizational Characteristics. SRNPs stand out in that their mission or primary activity is much more likely to be child care provision than is the case for other types of nonprofits. More than one quarter (28 percent) of the SRNPs were child care centers or preschools, a slightly higher proportion

TABLE 16.1   Nonprofit Organizations in Illinois: Characteristics by Size[a] and Religious Affiliation

	Small Religious Nonprofits	Small Secular Nonprofits	Large Religious Nonprofits	Large Secular Nonprofits	Total Sample
Organizational characteristics					
Child care/preschool as primary mission	28%[b]	11	—[c]	—	11
Target services to low/moderate income populations	14	26	32	11	21
Founded since 1980	24	34	4	4	24
Not on IRS Master List	27	10	16	10	13
Financial characteristics					
Less than $100,000 in annual revenue	51	44	—[d]	—	32
More than half of revenue from:					
Government	5	22	38	68	32
Donations	40	37	16	5	29
Fees	40	21	29	14	22
Show an operating loss in prior fiscal year	32	30	38	27	30
Either break even or show a surplus up to 10% of annual expenditures	43	47	59	58	50
Assets of 10% or less of annual expenditures	29	25	10	9	21
Assets of 76% or more of annual expenditures	22	28	59	39	32
Have budget planning features	17	22	38	42	27
Rent space from religious congregations	10	9	34	9	11
Borrow space from religious congregations	47	13	21	10	18
Value of donated space from congregations as % of total revenues	6.6	2.2	0.3	0.0	2.2

NOTES: a. "Small" nonprofits have annual expenditures of less than $500,000 or fewer than 20 full-time equivalent staff.
b. The numbers in this table give the percentage of each type of organization with the specified characteristic. For example, 28% of SRNPs have child care or preschool as their primary mission. The sample is weighted to correct for disproportionately low response rates from both the smallest and the largest organizations. One-way analysis of variance was performed for each variable in this table. With one exception, differences among these four types of organizations are significant at least at the .01 level. These four types of organizations are not significantly different from each other in their likelihood of showing an operating loss or surplus.
c. Only three large nonprofits of either religious or secular affiliation have child care or preschool as their primary mission.
d. By definition, no large nonprofits have annual revenues under $500,000.

than for other small nonprofits (11 percent), even though Catholic-affiliated centers are absent from this sample. SRNPs are about as likely as other non-profits to engage in other sorts of primary activities. Twenty-eight percent of SRNPs report their primary mission as human services, followed by health-related services (12 percent), community development or advocacy organizations (9 percent), and residential facilities (5 percent).

We asked organizations whether they particularly targeted their programs or services to ethnic minorities or to people of low to moderate income. Surprisingly, hardly any SRNPs (4 percent) report that they target a minority group, and only 14 percent target low- or moderate-income groups. SRNPs are not different from other organizations in their likelihood of aiming their services at minority groups, but they are significantly less likely than other organizations to direct their services specifically to the economically disprivileged. As Table 16.1 shows, only 14 percent of SRNPs target low- and moderate-income groups—a rate comparable to that of large secular non-profits—while 26 percent and 32 percent, respectively, of small secular non-profits and large religious nonprofits target the economically disprivileged.

Small nonprofits, regardless of religious affiliation, are younger than large nonprofits. One quarter (24 percent) of SRNPs were established after 1980; an additional 42 percent were founded during the 1970s. Small secular nonprofits have even higher rates of recent establishment: 34 percent since 1980 and another 35 percent in the 1970s. By contrast, only 4 percent of large nonprofits have been founded since 1980.

As we mentioned above, SRNPs are less likely to obtain official IRS tax-exempt status. Fully 27 percent of SRNPs were not included on the IRS listing, a substantially higher proportion than for other small nonprofits (10 percent) or for large organizations, either religious (16 percent) or secular (10 percent). Most of this difference is because SRNP child care centers and preschools are especially likely (65 percent) to be excluded from the IRS list. They differ significantly on this dimension both from similar agencies without religious affiliation and from other SRNPs. Most likely, this percentage would have been even higher had Catholic-affiliated child care centers and preschools been included in our sample.

Financial Characteristics. Average *expenditures* for SRNPs in our sample were $198,000, about 20 percent smaller than for other small nonprofits ($243,000). The spread between the two groups is somewhat smaller for average *revenues:* $215,000 versus $253,000. Neither difference is statistically significant. As shown in Table 16.1, however, SRNPs are more likely than other small nonprofits to be *very* small (annual revenue under

$100,000). This difference is especially pronounced for religiously affiliated child care centers and preschools, 81 percent of which are very small, compared to 40 percent of secular child care centers and preschools. This difference may be related to the fact that SRNP child care centers and preschools are much more likely to be housed in churches or synagogues than are secular nonprofits of the same sort.

Another reason why SRNP child care centers or preschools are so small may be that they rarely have access to government funding, a major source of growth for many nonprofit human service organizations. Virtually all (94 percent) of the SRNP child care/preschool organizations obtained the majority of their revenues from fees; only 59 percent of secular child care/preschool organizations did so. A substantial proportion (38 percent) of the latter group obtained at least half of their revenues from government sources. Only 6 percent of religiously affiliated child care centers and preschools obtained more than half their revenues from public funds.

Table 16.1 shows patterns in revenue sources for all four organizational types. Though less pronounced than for the child care/preschool comparison described in the previous paragraph, the basic pattern is the same. Religious nonprofits, and especially small religious nonprofits, are more reliant on fees and less reliant on public funds than are other types of organizations. Given commonplace interpretations of the constitutional separation between church and state, this is not a surprising pattern. Recent efforts to make government funding available to churches for the delivery of human services may change these configurations.

In order to provide a reasonable basis for comparing the financial health of SRNPs, we computed annual surplus and total assets as percentages of total expenditures for the fiscal year. As Table 16.1 shows, one third (32 percent) of SRNPs reported an operating loss in the prior fiscal year, and another 43 percent either broke even or had a surplus equivalent to no more than 10 percent of total expenditures. Only 25 percent had a more substantial surplus. Interestingly, there are no significant differences here among various types of nonprofits. In terms of financial surpluses, religious nonprofits in general and SRNPs in particular appear to be no worse (or better) off than other nonprofits.

Assets present a somewhat different story. Here, the main effect is size. As Table 16.1 shows, larger organizations do significantly better across the board. Controlling for size, religiously affiliated nonprofits have neither greater nor lesser assets than secular nonprofits. We should mention, however, that, in terms of assets, SRNP child care centers and preschools are most vulnerable, probably because they are more likely to be very small and housed in congregations. Almost half (48 percent) have net assets equivalent to at best 10 percent of total expenditures, compared to 26 percent for small secular child care centers and preschools.

We use two simple planning features to determine the extent to which organizations plan their budgets: whether they distinguish between capital and operating funds and whether they have established a reserve fund in their operating budget for maintenance expenditures. Nagle (1994) found for child care agencies that these features are closely related to more general planning capacity and that they are also associated with larger size and receipt of restricted funding, such as government support. Table 16.1 gives the percentage of each type of organization with both of these planning tools in place. Small nonprofits are substantially less likely to have both of these planning features in place, and small religious nonprofits are least likely to have them. Here, again, SRNP child care centers and preschools are particularly vulnerable. Only 6 percent have both of these planning features in place, compared with 25 percent for small secular child care centers and preschools.

Very few (10 percent) SRNPs lease space from congregations, but 47 percent use space donated by them. This is particularly the case for SRNP child care centers and preschools (85 percent). This is an important finding, since child care centers and preschools are facility-intensive organizations and require access to particular types of space that meet state and city licensing and/or safety standards. Indeed, other research has shown that as many as one third of the nation's child care centers are located within congregations (Community Workshop on Economic Development [CWED] 1991; Lindner, Mattis, and Rogers 1983). While relatively few (about 10 percent) non-SRNPs borrow space from congregations, more rent from them, especially large religiously affiliated agencies (34 percent) and small child care centers and preschools without religious affiliations (21 percent).

The average SRNP receives about $5,800 of donated space from religious congregations, compared to about $2,000 for small secular nonprofits, about $4,100 for large religious nonprofits, and about $500 for large secular nonprofits.[2] Considering all sources of donated space, small secular nonprofits benefit more than small religious nonprofits, receiving free space valued at, on average, 10.8 percent of their total revenue, compared to 7.3 percent for

---

2   To estimate the value of donated space, we use the median rent per square foot paid by each functionally specific type of agency (i.e., child care and preschool agencies, human and residential care agencies, and "others") that rents space. Using one-way analysis of variance, the reported differences in the monetary value of donated space among the four types of nonprofits are statistically significant at the .10 level.

SRNPs. As shown in Table 16.1, however, SRNPs use congregationally donated space to a greater extent than any other type of organization, receiving 6.6 percent of their total revenue in free space, as compared to 2.2 percent for small secular nonprofits.

To summarize, we have compared SRNPs both to small secular nonprofits and to large nonprofits, and we have been able to identify certain distinguishing characteristics of this organizational population, some of which are produced by smallness, others of which appear more directly related to religious affiliation. Small nonprofits, regardless of religious affiliation, are younger, less likely to receive more than half their revenue from the government, less likely to hold large assets, more likely to get free space from some source, and less likely to have institutionalized budget planning tools. Small *religious* organizations are more likely to be child care providers or preschools, less likely to target their services to the economically disprivileged, less likely to be officially registered with the IRS as nonprofit organizations, less likely to receive significant income from government sources, and more likely to operate in space donated by congregations.

PRACTICAL CONCLUSIONS

Our results point to several important conclusions, both for those who manage SRNPs and for those who would like to help them improve their material situation.

1. A special niche currently occupied by SRNPs is provision of child care and preschool education. Given the increasing importance of organizationally provided child care to American families, and given the large presence of SRNPs among such organizations, the particular resource vulnerabilities of SRNP child care centers and preschools—low levels of assets and inadequate planning capacity—are especially crucial needs to address.

2. SRNPs, especially child care centers and preschools, are hugely dependent on borrowed space, especially from congregations. This dependence makes them especially vulnerable to changes in the fortunes of urban congregations. Reducing this facilities dependence would help to stabilize SRNP's material resource situation.

3. Notwithstanding commonplace interpretations of the First Amendment, SRNPs probably could obtain higher levels of public support for their social service activities than they currently receive. SRNP leaders could be

educated on how to seek public support for these activities, mainly via separately incorporating their human service programs.

4. Relatedly, religious organizations in general and SRNPs in particular are less likely than other organizations to obtain official tax-exempt status by registering with the IRS. Although the reasons for this are unclear, the failure to obtain official IRS tax-exempt status can have significant resource consequences for SRNPs. In addition to forgoing the benefits of sales tax exemption when buying materials, both government funders and private foundations often require that recipients of their funds be incorporated as 501(c)(3) organizations. Failure to obtain this designation therefore greatly constricts a nonprofit organization's resource options. This point is reinforced by results reported in Chapter 17 of this volume.

REFERENCES

Community Workshop on Economic Development (CWED). 1991. *Good Space and Good Work: Research and Analysis of the Extent and Nature of the Use of Religious Properties in Chicago Neighborhoods.* Chicago: Inspired Partnerships Program of the National Trust for Historic Preservation in the United States.

Grønbjerg, Kirsten A. 1994. "The NTEE: Human Service and Regional Applications." *Voluntas* 5(3):301-28.

Grønbjerg, Kirsten A., and Sheila Nelson. 1998. "Mapping Small Religious Nonprofit Organizations: An Illinois Profile." *Nonprofit and Voluntary Sector Quarterly* 27:13-31.

Human Care Services Directory of Metropolitan Chicago, 1991-1992. 1992. Chicago: United Way/Crusade of Mercy.

Lindner, E. W., M. C. Mattis, and J. R. Rogers. 1993. *When Churches Mind the Children: A Study of Day Care in Local Parishes.* Ypsilanti, MI: High Scope Press.

Nagle, Ami. 1994. "Nonprofit Child Care Facility Management: Funding Reliance, Size, and Organization Behavior." M.A. thesis, Department of Sociology and Anthropology, Loyola University, Chicago.

Chapter 17

Philanthropic Institutions and the Small Religious Nonprofit

ELLEN J. BENJAMIN

This chapter focuses on private grantmaking institutions' practices and perceptions that hinder, usually unintentionally, small religious organizations' efforts to obtain resources from such institutions. Specifically, this chapter describes current behaviors that influence relations between philanthropic organizations and small religious nonprofits (SRNPs), identifies specific areas of misperception and misunderstanding, and delineates activities that might diminish barriers and forge partnerships between SRNPs and potential donors. As in Chapter 16 of this volume, SRNP means nonprofit social service and advocacy programs that are both religious and small. Unlike in Chapter 16, however, I include under the SRNP rubric social service and advocacy programs that are *not* separately incorporated from a larger sponsoring church, synagogue, mosque, or other religious institution. The focus here is therefore on funding opportunities for activities and programs that may or may not themselves be under the purview of a formal organization separate from a sponsoring religious organization.

Data on which this chapter is based come from a mail survey of grant-making institutions associated with the Donors Forum of Chicago. The Donors Forum of Chicago is a regional association of grantmaking organizations whose diverse membership includes family, independent, community, and corporate foundations, as well as companies with philanthropic giving programs. Completed questionnaires were received from 72 of the 150 grantmakers (48 percent) associated with the Forum.

This chapter documents the ways in which grantmaker perceptions, expectations, and practices clash with the organizational realities of SRNP activities. Although grantmakers exhibit substantial interest and goodwill toward SRNPs, there exists a vast gulf between, on the one hand, the knowledge, expectations, and practices of donors and, on the other hand, the organizational realities of SRNPs. As a consequence, SRNPs unnecessarily miss out on funding opportunities, and donors unnecessarily overlook grantmaking opportunities. At the same time, there is good reason to believe that these problems may be addressed through education and enhanced communication. The next section presents some basic findings from this research; a concluding section mentions seven practical conclusions that emerge from this work. Readers interested in more methodological or substantive detail should see the article by Benjamin (1997), from which this chapter is adapted.

FINDINGS

Misunderstandings. More than just conscience guides the distribution of philanthropy. Although foundations may select grantees from among eligible recipients, all donors must abide by rules that define permissibility for charitable gifts. Statutes, decrees, and cases establishing these rules come from a variety of sources, the most important of which are the Internal Revenue Service, the U.S. Congress, and the federal courts. Perhaps because of the complexity of the regulatory environment, it is sometimes incorrectly assumed that it is illegal for private funders to make grants to religious organizations (Troyer, Boisture, and Livingston 1993:1). In fact, legally, private funders are entirely free to support religious activities in America.

Foundations operating under broad charters permitting support to charitable endeavors may make grants to religious institutions without any limitation, whether for worship and proselytizing or for the types of social service, advocacy, and educational activities typically carried out by SRNPs. Likewise, grantmaking organizations restricted by their charter to the promotion of a particular cause, such as child welfare, are free to fund religiously affiliated programs that are relevant to their mission—for example, group homes, foster care agencies, and adoption assistance programs. Furthermore, even those foundation charters prohibiting the advancement of religion leave grantmakers free to support religious organizations engaged in secular activities. Hence, great latitude is afforded in the United States for private philanthropic support of religiously affiliated human services.

At least among Chicago grantmakers, this categorical latitude is well understood. Only 2 percent of the grantmakers responding to this survey inaccurately believed it to be illegal for private foundations or corporations to provide grants to churches, mosques, synagogues, and other religious organizations.

Notwithstanding their grasp of the basic legal permissibility of support for religious organizations, many donors believe that religious organizations are uncontrollable in ways that may make them less desirable grant recipients. One cause of this confusion is some donors' mistaken belief that the U.S. Constitution's guarantee of the free exercise of religion applies to them. But, of course, the First Amendment does not restrict grantmaker operations, and private grantmakers are free to place conditions on grants made to religious organizations in precisely the same manner, and to the same extent, that they may restrict grants to secular grantees. It is entirely within the rights of grantmakers to require that an SRNP comply with specified standards of financial accounting reporting, not use more than a stated percentage of a grant for overhead expenses, provide public acknowledgment of a grant, or serve all who walk in the door.

This fact is not, however, well understood. As shown in Table 17.1, 32 percent of the private grantmakers responding to this study did not know if they could place requirements (such as nondiscrimination) upon SRNPs, and 7 percent incorrectly believed that they could not. This means that more than a third of private grantmakers are at least uncertain about their ability to insist on the same stipulations from religiously affiliated nonprofits that would typically be required of secular recipients. This is important because fundamental to the operation of most private grantmakers is the deeply held belief that they are and should be free to award support according to whatever criteria they choose to use and in line with whatever restrictions they see fit to impose. Applicants perceived to be less subject to donor preferences and less amenable to conforming to donor guidelines rarely will be provided funding. The misperception that religious organizations are, in general, of this sort raises a barrier to funding that need not exist.

Table 17.1 presents other findings about grantmakers' perceptions of religious organizations. These results show that donors commonly misunder-

TABLE 17.1 Grantmakers' Perceptions of Religious Organizations

	Grantmakers' Opinions		
	True (%)	False (%)	No Opinion (%)
It is impossible for private foundations and corporations to place requirements on religious organizations that they may place on secular grantees.	7	61*	32
Religious institutions and organizations are exempt from applying for IRS tax-exempt status.	14*	61	25
Religious institutions and organizations are required to file tax returns with the IRS.	47	25*	28
Many religious organizations are affiliated with religious denominations that have applied for so-called group rulings from the IRS that acknowledge tax-exempt and public charity status.	67*	7	26
If a private foundation or corporation supports an SRNP, this might be interpreted as endorsing the recipient's religious beliefs.	45	44	11

NOTE: *Correct answer.

stand the regulatory environment faced by religious organizations. Two regulatory misunderstandings are particularly important. The first is that only 14 percent of grantmakers correctly recognized that religious organizations are exempt from the general requirement that organizations must apply to the IRS to obtain tax-exempt status. The second is that only 25 percent of responding grantmakers correctly recognized that many religious organizations are not required to file tax returns. In fact, religious organizations are not obliged to file tax returns, nor must they apply to the Internal Revenue Service for a determination of their "public charity" status. The majority of grantmakers apparently misunderstand this situation.

A third regulatory misunderstanding, though less prevalent than the first two, is still worth mentioning. Only two thirds of grantmakers are aware that most churches are covered by group exemption rulings obtained by their convention or denomination. In the case of a prospective grantee covered by a denominational group exemption ruling, grantmakers may confirm status as a tax-exempt public charity by obtaining a copy of the group ruling and of the grantee's listing in the official denominational directory or comparable listing of organizations covered by the group ruling.

TABLE 17.2 Factors Influencing Funding Decisions According to Grantmakers

Percentage of Grantmakers Saying Factor:	*Will Encourage Funding*	*Will Discourage Funding*	*Will Have No Impact on Funding*	*Don't Know*
What impact will it have on funding if:				
A nonprofit does not have its own 501(c)(3) status?	0	75	21	4
A program is less than three years old?	17	44	32	7
A program has not yet received support from other foundations or corporations?	1	66	27	6
A religious leader is spokesperson for a potential grantee?	9	30	44	17
Supported services will be housed in a religious institution?	4	36	46	14
A proposal narrative conveys a religious philosophy underpinning an organization's mission?	7	59	14	20
Oversight is provided by a religious institution's trustees rather than by an independent board?	0	59	20	21
A solicitor is unknown to the foundation or corporation from which funds are sought?	4	43	45	8

These misunderstandings imply that grantmakers do not, in general, realize how their documentation requirements unintentially and unnecessarily exclude many SRNPs from the ranks of potential grantees. It is common practice for grantmakers to assess whether an organization is qualified as a tax-exempt public charity (and, therefore, legally eligible for a contribution) by requesting a copy of the applicant's IRS ruling on their status. Similarly, for many donors, submission of a tax return is a nonnegotiable requirement during the grant review process. As shown in Table 17.2, fully 75 percent of grantmakers in this survey report that support is less likely to be forthcoming when applicants do not have their own 501(c)(3) status.

Taken together, these results suggest that there is substantial misunderstanding by grantmakers regarding the laws that govern SRNP legal status, the documentation available to substantiate an SRNP as a legal grant recipient, and SRNPs' legal openness to meeting donor guidelines. The result is that funders may inadvertently penalize SRNPs that, for example, might be unable to provide documentation that is standardly available from secular organizations performing the same activities. This documentation barrier will be especially high when it comes to funding congregation-based programs and activities that are not under the purview of a separately incorporated organization.

Grantmaker Expectations and SRNP Practices and Characteristics. In addition to missed opportunities arising from donor misunderstanding about religious organizations' reporting requirements, there are ways in which common SRNP practices typically fail to match grantmaker expectations. For example, some SRNP leaders believe, as a point of principle, that they should focus on their mission, not on their finances; these SRNPs may intentionally remain inattentive to fiscal matters and may not want to devote time to drafting budget materials. More commonly, SRNPs that would be willing to develop income and expense reports simply have no information from which to create clear reports because they have not separated their accounting records from those of their sponsoring religious institution.

SRNP practices making it difficult to develop a budget present a high obstacle to obtaining external funds. Donors are loathe to supply monies to an institution that cannot provide documentation of financial planning and management, and they are likely to reject otherwise sound proposals on this basis alone. A full 69 percent of Chicago grantmakers report that they will "rarely" provide a grant if prior, current, and projected program budgets are not included in a proposal. Another 28 percent will only "sometimes" provide a grant under such circumstances.

Two other characteristics common among SRNPs—newness and relative isolation from the foundation world—erect further barriers between their social service activities and funding. As shown in Table 17.2, 44 percent of grantmakers in this sample say that the likelihood of funding is reduced if a program is less than three years old, and 66 percent say that not receiving prior support from a foundation or corporation will count against an SRNP's request for funding.

Reticence About Religion. Regulatory misunderstandings and mismatched budget practices are not the only ways in which SRNPs experience incongruity with the philanthropic community. Grantmakers also manifest a certain discomfort with explicit religious goals and commitments. Table 17.2 presents relevant results. Thirty percent of grantmakers in this sample report that having a religious leader as spokesperson for a nonprofit activity reduces the likelihood of support; 36 percent say that housing an activity in a religious institution discourages support for that activity; a majority—59 percent—report that the likelihood of support is reduced if a proposal narrative conveys a religious philosophy underpinning the nonprofit's mission; and a majority—again 59 percent—report that support is less likely if oversight of the activity is provided by a religious institution's board of trustees rather than by an independent board whose sole focus is on the provision of social services.

The reason for this discomfort with explicit religious identity or commitment appears to be that grantmakers are reluctant to appear to be supporting *religious* activities. Forty-five percent of grantmakers in this survey say that if a private foundation or corporation provides support for secular human services offered by a church, mosque, synagogue, or other religious organization, this might be interpreted as endorsing the recipient's core religious beliefs and functions. The desire to avoid this perception seems to constitute a strong barrier between foundations and SRNPs.

Overall, the findings from this study suggest that, as a subset of all nonprofits, SRNPs confront obstacles in the effort to obtain foundation funding for their activities. Some of these obstacles—for example, the difficulty posed by never having received foundation support—are shared with small secular nonprofits. Other obstacles—for example, donors' apparent reluctance to appear to be supporting religion and the greater likelihood of religiously based activities not to reside in a separately incorporated organizations—are peculiar to small *religious* nonprofits. None of these obstacles, however, is necessarily insurmountable, and the concluding section offers concrete suggestions for overcoming them.

PRACTICAL CONCLUSIONS

Although this research has been designed to generate knowledge about the preferences, practices, and assumptions of potential donors that will be helpful to SRNPs, I do not mean to imply that all SRNPs should *want* to seek out this funding and alter their practices accordingly. There is always the possibility that changes made to accommodate a donor's preferences will either conflict with the core religious values of an SRNP or alienate its religious base. It may be that doing what is necessary to obtain foundation funding will involve trading one set of problems for another. Leaders of SRNPs will have to evaluate these trade-offs for themselves. The following practical suggestions are offered for those who decide that foundation funding is worth pursuing. Some of these point out ways SRNPs can help to educate misinformed donors, while others point to organizational changes that can improve the chances for support.

1. If independent 501(c)(3) status has not been obtained, consider developing an autonomous governing council and perhaps seeking autonomous incorporation of activities for which outside support is sought.

2. Seek technical training in grantwriting, budget preparation, and other aspects of nonprofit management from organizations (e.g., United Way, the Executive Service Corps and Support Center) that provide such support.

3. Establish systems for maintaining full fiscal records (apart from those kept by a sponsoring religious organization) and prepare to share this information with potential donors.

4. Submit grant applications that include a clear explanation of deductibility status as well as an explanation of the role that theology and religious practices play in the delivery of social services.

5. Where possible, explicitly indicate your willingness to comply with donor preferences and guidelines.

6. A very important way to overcome both donor misunderstanding and possible reticence about religiously based activities is to establish personal contact with potential grantmakers. Fifty-one percent of grantmakers in this study reported that a visit with a potential recipient is "frequently" or "always" influential in deciding whether or not to offer support; another 31 percent said that such a meeting is "sometimes" influential. Also relevant here is the finding that 43 percent of grantmakers said that a proposal from a group that is unknown to the foundation will reduce the likelihood of funding. This leads to a concrete suggestion: Set up meetings with funders promptly after making a solicitation.

7. Be persistent and ambitious. As described above, initial support from a donor is likely to breed further fund-raising success.

REFERENCES

Benjamin, Ellen J. 1997. "Philanthropic Institutions and the Small Religious Nonprofit." *Nonprofit and Voluntary Sector Quarterly* 26:S29-S43.

Troyer, Thomas A., Robert Boisture, and Catherine Livingston. 1993. *MEMORANDUM: Legal Considerations Affecting Public and Private Grantmaking to Religious Organizations.* Washington, DC: Council on Foundations.

PART **IV**

CONCLUSION

Chapter **18**

Faith and Money

Theological Reflections on Financing American Religion

JOHN M. MULDER

Until very recently, we have known very little about the financing of American religion, despite religion's billion-dollar status in the American economy and despite the critical importance of material resources to the health and vitality of religious institutions. The chapters in this book start to fill the void. They represent pioneering work that explores the least studied area of American religious life and, together, they address both the material and the spiritual condition of American churches.

This body of work raises questions about money and about the financing of American religion that should be addressed by theologians, clergy, laypeople, and the churches themselves. In this chapter, I reflect theologically on these chapters by identifying and discussing nine such questions.

WHAT IS MONEY?

There is pervasive confusion in American society about the definition of money, and churches do not seem to be addressing this confusion very effectively. Clearly, money makes possible the provision of commodities and services, perpetuates institutions, and advances the mission of the church. In the contemporary American economy, and certainly earlier as well, money also connects intimately with definitions of the self. Defining one's life involves one's income. Despite money's central importance to our lives, discussion of it is "taboo" (a concept with its own suggestive theological implications). The sense of money as taboo is reinforced by themes in the Christian tradition that criticize acquisition, celebrate the ascetic, and set faith against culture. Three points seem pertinent here.

First, the power of "money" is a relatively recent development in economic history, dating to the rise of capitalism in the seventeenth century. Money, economists tell us, is animated. It has "life," "velocity," and "momentum." These metaphors suggest that money, whatever else it is, is not mundane. The autonomous, even metaphysical, character of money deserves sustained theological and ethical reflection.

Second, American culture contains a strong "money is negative" theme. This is especially evident in parts of our religious culture. The love of money, one passage in the Bible tells us, is the root of all evil, and an overwhelming majority of Americans believe we are too materialistic. This theme contains problematic theological and historical assumptions. One is that the Christian tradition is generally hostile to money and to culture generally, an assumption that obscures many other themes in Christian theology that emphasize the goodness of creation or the centrality of redemption in Christ. Another is the tendency to operate with ideal and polarized categories—in this case the spiritual versus the material. Although certain movements in the history of the church have posed the issue in such stark terms, there are other, rich options upon which to draw. If nothing else, the doctrine of the incarnation—God becoming human, the spiritual becoming material—raises serious obstacles to defining the Christian life as a matter of mutually exclusive categories of existence.

Third, the undefined and largely undiscussed character of money raises the question of whether giving money is different from other forms of giving. The Christian tradition suggests that it is. When Jesus says, "Where your treasure is, there will your heart be also," he is drawing the connection between money and human identity. If money and human life are intimately woven together, then giving money is giving away oneself.

Some research, especially that in Chapters 1, 3, and 9, points out that giving money should be placed in the context of the tremendous amount of time that religious people give to churches and other charitable causes. Still, donating time to a cause is not laden with the same powerful inhibitions and rewards as is the giving of money. How we conceive of money has profound implications for how we interpret theologically the act of giving itself, especially the giving of money, and the gift of money thereby raises significant theological questions about the nature of Christian discipleship.

WHO GIVES MONEY TO CHURCHES?

Research reported in this volume, especially in Chapters 1 and 3, is especially informative on this question, confirming some hypotheses and refuting others. The rich give the most, but lower-income people give higher percentages of their income. Protestants give more than Catholics, but Catholics are not inhibited because of dissatisfaction with their church. Conservative Protestants give more than moderate or liberal Protestants, yet there also are significant differences among theologically similar denominations. Individuals and congregations increasingly support local and designated causes, rather than national and international causes advocated by denominations.

Understudied, however, is the role of gender in giving. We know that American churches are composed of a majority of women in all denominations, so it would not come as a surprise to learn that women are the primary source of religious philanthropy in the United States, but this has not yet been documented. (I will have more to say about gender in the Conclusion.)

Similarly, although the research described by Calvin Pressley and Walter Collier in Chapter 3 suggests that giving among African Americans is similar in important respects to giving among whites, the dynamics of giving in these churches—not to mention giving among Hispanics and other ethnic religious communities—surely warrants further exploration to give us a more nuanced understanding of the diversity of religious philanthropy.

The *theological* question arising here, however, is whether gender, race, and ethnicity have any theological import. Future inquiry should go beyond the now expected affirmation of distinctive roles and behaviors based on gender and ethnicity. Instead, theologians should be encouraged to pursue the constructive theological task of asking what these groups offer as a vision of understanding money, giving, and the Christian life.

WHY DO PEOPLE GIVE
MONEY TO CHURCHES?

Some of this research, especially Sharon Miller's Chapter 5, speaks to this question of motivation. For some, giving money to the church is a discipline—a duty to provide for the perpetuation and strengthening of the church. For others, it is a means of providing for services and mission in which they believe. Still others perceive giving to the church as a reciprocal relationship: returning to God a portion of what God has given to them or seeking further blessing from God by supporting the church. At least two theological issues are raised by these findings.

First, all of these motivations tend to revolve around the confusing and often contradictory meaning of "stewardship." Further, they are based on a conception of stewardship rooted in the Christian doctrine of creation. God created the world; we are God's stewards; therefore, we give back to God what has been entrusted to us. Notably missing from the expressed motivations of most people who give to churches is one rooted in Christology: because of God's salvation in Jesus Christ, I respond in gratitude and give my money to God and the church.

Second, this research, especially in Chapters 8, 10, and 11, uncovers the studied silence about money in the church. Most ministers claim they have preached about money or stewardship during the course of a year, but ironically most laypeople cannot remember hearing such sermons. It should scarcely be surprising that theology does not play a significant role in shaping the motivation of why people give money to the church.

Nevertheless, the findings about motivation have definite theological implications. At the very least, this information should prompt us to ask why pastors are so reluctant to speak about money and stewardship and why people so resist hearing them address this issue. But we should also explore redefining "stewardship" to expand its base beyond the confines of the doctrine of creation. If giving money to the church could be reinterpreted as an expression of grace and forgiveness, it might mitigate the legalism and moralism that sometimes characterize and curse the discussions of money in the life of the church.

WHY DO SOME PEOPLE GIVE MORE MONEY TO CHURCHES THAN OTHERS?

Several chapters provide answers to this question. To me, the two most interesting patterns are that Protestants give more than Catholics and conservative Protestants give more than moderate or liberal Protestants. The explanation for the disparity between Protestants and Catholics seems to lie in the relative absence of emphasis on stewardship and giving in Catholic parishes, at least until relatively recently. The difference between conservative and moderate or liberal Protestantism apparently is explained by "commitment" and "evangelical theology."

These differences raise interesting theological questions. For instance, is there something about Protestant theology that stimulates giving? In contrast, are there themes in Catholic theology that may work against giving to the church? Similarly, it would be interesting to reflect on why conservative or evangelical Protestant theology seems to prompt higher levels of giving to the church. Might an emphasis on Christology and salvation be a factor? Or, is the focus on the work of the Holy Spirit an important influence? Or, as the Ronsvalles suggest in Chapter 2, is a greater emphasis on missions the stimulus to greater generosity?

Theological analysis of why people give differently will not only enhance our understanding of religious philanthropy. It will also stimulate the task of constructing a theology about money, philanthropy, and the Christian life in which we can draw on the insights of other traditions.

WHAT IS THE CHURCH?

Denominations are facing a fiscal revolution. As the Ronsvalles make clear in Chapter 2, congregations are keeping more money for their own programs, local needs, and designated mission. Less and less money is sent to governing bodies of the denominations, especially the national structures. A complementary development is the rise and power of nondenominational parachurch organizations. Although these organizations apparently confront financial anxieties of their own, as described in Chapter 14, they are relatively robust and healthy in comparison to national denominational structures. Much ink has been spilled on what this might mean for the future—networks replacing denominational agencies, decentralization of mission activity, denominational agencies restructured to serve congregations rather than vice versa, and so on. What has not been addressed very widely is what this fiscal revolution means for the doctrine of the church.

The historian Sidney Mead has been fond of criticizing the Christian churches in the United States for failing to deal with the theological conflict created by accepting the pluralism of denominationalism while simultaneously clinging to the uniqueness of Christianity. There is a similar theological conflict in recognizing that churches are voluntary organizations in American society and yet affirming that the church is God's gift to us, rather than our gift to God. If localism, individualism, and choice are in fact fueling the fiscal revolution in American churches, and if congregational initiatives will shape the future of Christianity in American society, the concept of the church as a corporate entity—the body of Christ—and a vision of mission beyond one's own community may be imperiled. I believe that the doctrine of the church has emerged as an issue that deserves urgent and creative discussion. It may be the most important theological issue to emerge from this body of research.

WHY SHOULD PEOPLE GIVE
MONEY TO THE CHURCH?

In his historical survey of mainline Protestant attitudes toward faith and money, Robert Lynn notes in Chapter 7 that a continuous theme is the attempt to discuss the authority by which the church asks for money. The responses have varied, he says, and by the late twentieth century this tradition has become virtually mute about why people should financially support a church. Why people should give money to the church is a constructive, normative issue that ought to engage theologians. Obviously embedded in this inquiry is the authority of Christianity itself—perhaps the most fundamental challenge to Christian belief in a postmodern world.

Churches can hardly be expected to answer the question of authority for its financial appeals without being able to address the question of authority for its claims to truth. Moreover, the issue of authority has two critical dimensions for theological reflection. It is not only the question of authority for truth claims but the authority of the church as an institution. Since huge majorities of Americans, both inside and outside the churches, believe that an individual can and should arrive at religious truth without regard for church teachings or church membership, the authority of the church as an institution is in question. C. S. Lewis called his apologia *The Case for Christianity*. We need people who will make "a case for the church."

HOW MUCH MONEY SHOULD
PEOPLE GIVE TO THE CHURCH?

This question arises repeatedly in these chapters, and both Robert Lynn's and James Hudnut-Beumler's historical overviews make it clear that this is not a new issue in the history of American Protestantism. The question involves the precarious status of the "tithe" and its theological justification, as well as "proportional giving" and other guidelines for religious philanthropy. At first glance, this may seem a debate about tactics and strategies involved in garnering support for the church, but I believe the problem is deeper than that. The question of how much money should be given to the church is a direct corollary of the theological question: What is the church and what is its authority? This question assumes even more urgency in a culture where the church is "disestablished" and where churches compete for the allegiance, time, values, and money of its members.

Few will say that all of an individual's philanthropy should be directed to the church or even to a specific congregation. There are too many worthwhile causes that need support, and no single congregation or even denomination can embrace the scope of what the Christian discipline of giving money might include. In this regard, research on giving tends to contain a troubling distinction between "religious" and "nonreligious" giving or the support of "religious" and "nonreligious" causes. Although this distinction may be helpful in discerning the full scope of an individual's philanthropic interest, theologically it suggests the compartmentalization of existence that the Christian tradition would largely reject. The question of balancing conflicting interests and values has been an enduring theme in philosophy and theology since the ancient Greeks. How much money people should give to the church, and how to allocate giving among available worthy alternatives, are questions that ought to engage theologians.

These also are questions with urgent implications for ministry and pastoral care. Both pastors and their congregations yearn for counsel about how to balance the conflicting demands on their money and their lives. One friend of mine has told me that he is "eternally grateful" for my advice about how to divide his estate between the interests of his children and his lifelong charitable interests. Raising and giving money is basically a matter of pastoral care: trying to get one's values and one's money going in the same direction, when too often they diverge.

WHAT IS AND WHAT SHOULD BE THE RELATIONSHIP OF CLERGY TO MONEY AND THE GIVING OF MONEY?

As noted earlier, there is a powerful ambivalence about money in American life, an ambivalence reflected in the churches. I want to suggest that this ambivalence is not necessarily undesirable, something that we ought to eliminate from theological reflection and Christian practice. Instead, it ought to be seen as a creative tension in the Christian life and as an opportunity for exploring some of the critical components of Christian discipleship. For example, money is evil in its capacity to encourage people to define their existence in terms of how much they can accumulate. Money is good, however, in its power to provide the basics of life, to alleviate human suffering, to enhance beauty, to advance truth. Chapters 8 and 11 make clear that both Protestant and Catholic clergy avoid talking about money. If this is true, and if their parishioners often do not hear them even when they do preach and teach about money, then we are missing the creative possibilities inherent in ambivalence about money, and we need significant theological reflection and education that will help clergy create contexts in which people are liberated to speak about the deep fears and anxieties related to money.

Here Robert Wuthnow's argument in Chapter 8 about the present "crisis" in the church has considerable validity. Wuthnow maintains that the problems of American churches are both fiscal and spiritual. Clergy, he says, are not addressing the intersection between work, money, and faith. When the churches speak about economic issues, they tend to focus on the immorality and rapaciousness of corporations and abuses of capitalist societies. These indictments may be true, but they do not address the fear of those whose jobs may be eliminated or the angst of people caught in a system they cannot change.

Too often missing from preaching and teaching about money is theological and pastoral attention to the idea of vocation. What does it mean to be called by God? What does it mean to follow Christ? I recently did a literature search on *vocation* for an encyclopedia article, and I was struck by the absence of writing on this issue during the past 40 years. Vocation has virtually disappeared as a subject for theological reflection, and I believe the churches' silence about it has contributed to the spiritual and economic crisis of contemporary Christianity.

Emphasizing vocation will not resolve the ambivalence about money in Christianity, but it may provide a context for thinking about the conflicts money poses. It also offers an educational opportunity for people to examine how their call by God to be disciples of Christ might be related to their work and the income they earn. Addressing vocation may also be a means of opening up the doctrine of redemption as a source for theological reflection on money and the nature of commitment. A sense of commitment, after all, looms large in the profile of generous givers.

Two other issues regarding ministry deserve mention. First, contemporary clergy often identify more strongly with their congregations than with their denominations. Some clergy, in fact, are apathetic or even hostile to the needs of the denominations they serve. In the Presbyterian Church, this disaffection is particularly true of some pastors of large congregations—the congregations, not incidentally, where there is the greatest potential for increased benevolences.

I suspect that clerical alienation or apathy is, in fact, one reason for the dramatic reallocation of funds away from denominational programs to congregational needs and priorities. Perhaps clergy are not educating their congregations about denominational needs and priorities partly because of their own ambivalence about money or their fear of competition for the philanthropy of their members, but they might also resist because of their apathy about or alienation from their own denominational structures. None of these chapters explicitly explore ministerial alienation, but I want to suggest that the disaffection of clergy from their own church institutions is one piece of the larger complex of faith, money, and religious philanthropy.

Second, Daniel Conway, in Chapter 11, documents the absence of teaching about money, stewardship, and finances in theological education. Virtually all pastors and priests say that they had no instruction about these issues in seminary. The strange silence about money in the life of the church is matched by inattention to money and stewardship in theological seminary curricula.

The obvious implication is that something should be done about this, and something can be done. In this regard, the series on funding various types of parachurch organizations, published by the Christian Stewardship Association and summarized by Sharon Miller in Chapter 14, is a practical resource. These publications contain both useful information and practical guidance for raising money. If teaching about money enters the theological curriculum, however, I hope it will confront two challenges. First, courses should take seriously the historical and sociological literature so that students will understand the cultural context of churches and money in American life today. Second, these educational experiences should include sustained theological reflection about the themes raised in this literature and in the history of teaching about vocation and discipleship. Courses should not be designed only to provide practical guides to the raising of money, even though this is needed. Priests and pastors certainly need to know how to raise and manage money, but more important, they need to know why they should raise money and why people should give it to the church. Perhaps then ministers might even ask for it.

IS THERE A CRISIS IN FINANCING AMERICAN RELIGION?

I am not persuaded that there is a crisis in financing American religion. Let me use the Presbyterian Church (U.S.A.) as an example, even though it may be an exceptional case. Denominational funding from congregations has been declining since the 1950s. Today, the annual General Assembly budget is approximately $125 million. Seventy percent of that comes from endowment income and special offerings; only 30 percent comes from congregational benevolences. The church's foundation is adding millions of dollars in new gifts every year. Although endowment income traditionally has been spent only by General Assembly agencies, a new policy is in place to distribute these funds directly to local governing bodies. This looks less like a crisis and more like a fascinating process of institutional change.

Similarly, it is now clear that no denomination is capable of fully funding its theological seminaries. Only 3 percent of the budget at the seminary in which I work now comes from denominational support. Thirty years ago, 33 percent came from the denomination. And yet, as Anthony Ruger documents in Chapter 13, virtually all denominational seminaries, including ours, have raised sufficient annual support and endowment not only to survive but actually to expand educational programming. Where is the crisis? In my view, the language of crisis may actually be counterproductive in addressing the deep ambivalence in the churches about money and institutional change.

CONCLUSION

The body of research described in this volume tells us much about financing American religion. Of course, there is much more to learn. I conclude by pointing to four areas that seem to me particularly in need of additional work.

First, this body of work focuses exclusively on individuals and religious institutions in the United States. Clearly, there is an intimate connection between religious philanthropy, capitalism, and democratic political institutions. Take away either capitalism or democratic structures, and the nature of religious giving would be substantially different. Furthermore, the particular configuration of church and state in the United States has created distinctive, perhaps unique, patterns of religious philanthropy that certainly would look different in Italy or Britain or Kenya. Cross-national comparative research on financing religion would be very informative.

Second, although the historical work in Chapters 2, 6, and 7 constitutes a fine start, more is needed. We know next to nothing, for example, about the financial history of dioceses in the Catholic church, or about the changing patterns of religious giving in African American, Hispanic, and Asian congregations, or about how Protestant and Catholic missionary work was financed.

Third, as mentioned previously, we need more work on the role of women in financing American religion. Missions is one area in which we still know too little about the role of women, even though women largely financed Protestant missionary expansion of the nineteenth and early twentieth centuries. In the southern Presbyterian Church, the women's organization picked up the entire deficit of the church one year during the 1890s. I ran across an incident of a women's group in a Presbyterian congregation in Alabama where the bank was going to foreclose on the mortgage of the church during the Depression. The women's group paid off the mortgage. Women's orders in the Catholic church clearly have had a substantial economic impact, and both women's organizations in Protestantism and women's orders in Catholicism are undergoing dramatic change. All of these examples point to the need for more work that addresses the general question: What has been the financial role of women in American churches, and how is it changing?

Fourth, again picking up on points introduced earlier, additional theological work is needed on at least three broad themes: the nature of the church, vocation, and the nature of money and how much people should give.

Ecclesiology is a crucial doctrine in contemporary Christianity for a variety of reasons, only one of which is the changing financial pattern in contemporary religious life. The "disestablishment" of religion in American culture, the dramatic increase in religious pluralism, the changing character of mission, the increase in voluntarism and individualism—all these and more justify a fresh look at doctrines of the church. Included in any discussion of the nature of the church should be systematic and constructive attempts to answer questions about the church's authority and the church's mission. The discussion also should take place across traditions, rather than simply within various denominational groupings.

As indicated earlier, restoring the idea of vocation to an inquiry about money and the Christian life may be very helpful. It would provide a context for discussing the disjunction between faith and work that Wuthnow and others have discovered to be a pervasive issue in congregations. It also would provide an opportunity to bring the discussion of money and stewardship within a Christological framework.

Finally, normative questions about money and the giving of money pose fascinating and urgent theological and ethical issues for American churches—particularly in light of American society's affluence. These issues have not engaged the attention of theologians and ethicists in recent years; their attention has been focused more on a critique of capitalism and the nature of a just economic order. Redirecting attention to these problems will not be easy, but opening the discussion might lead to a broader vision of Christian discipleship.

Let me end where I began. The work described in this volume represents a pioneering effort to understand the financing of American religion. There is, as always, more to be done, but we have at least started down the path of developing a holistic understanding of the complex relationship between faith and money. Contemporary religious leaders will benefit from this understanding, and future researchers will be able to build on it.

Chapter 19

Financing
American Religion

MARK CHAVES

In the late 1980s and early 1990s, Religion Division staff at the Lilly Endowment began to hear from a variety of quarters that American religion was in financial crisis. Several national denominations were feeling the effects of declining resources. Small congregations seemed increasingly pinched by rising operating costs—from energy bills, to minimum salary requirements for clergy, to the pressure of old and decaying buildings. At the same time, the Religion Division received literally hundreds of requests for financial support, many with an air of desperation, from small religious nonprofit organizations across the country. Taken together, these and other signals seemed to point to a living concern of potentially profound importance for American religion, and a set of issues that no one really knew enough about to respond to with the necessary intelligence and creativity.

The Endowment's Financing of American Religion Initiative was an attempt to respond to this perception of financial crisis in American religion. The basic questions driving grantmaking in this initiative were of several sorts. Is there a crisis? If there is a financial crisis, is it a crisis of giving? How are the resource issues faced by congregations different from those faced by denominational entities, by theological schools, by religious elementary schools, by parachurch organizations, by small religious nonprofits? Are religious leaders equipped to manage the resources in their care? How is faith related to money and material resources? How has all of this changed over time?

These were some of the fundamental questions this initiative sought to answer, and it proceeded by building a body of research around the following more specific concerns. What are the trends in individual giving to congregations and why do some people give more than others? How do people relate—or fail to relate—their faith to their economic lives? What are the key aspects of the resource environments surrounding theological schools and Catholic parochial schools? What are the fund-raising challenges among various types of parachurch organizations? What are financial relationships between congregations and both regional and national judicatories? What are the management issues and practices in congregations with endowments and in religious nonprofit organizations? How do the financial activities and conditions of congregations compare to activities and conditions in the larger world of nonprofit organizations? How have the meanings of religious giving, and other aspects of religious financing, changed over time?

This volume has brought together the most significant research addressing these questions. In this concluding chapter, I present an overview of this body of work. This overview is based mainly on the preceding chapters, but it also is informed by the larger literature relevant to this area of inquiry. It is important to emphasize that this chapter represents my interpretation of this material; it is not intended as a summary of what has come before. It represents, instead, my own effort at synthesis.

This chapter has four parts. The first highlights the major findings to emerge from this body of work. There is a sense in which we know much more than I point to here, but I have tried to identify the most significant and solid pieces of knowledge. The second section highlights the major cross-cutting themes and questions presented by this body of work, and the third section identifies several sets of normative questions raised by these chapters. A fourth section describes several directions that future work might pursue. There is, inevitably, overlap among these sections, but I do not think there is redundancy. Some themes emerge in more than one section because they have more than one aspect.

WHAT DO WE KNOW?

Individual Giving

The heart of this body of work has been research on individual giving to religious organizations, especially congregations. Solid findings about individual giving have emerged, some but not all of which are well known. I group these findings into six sets. Most of this material is based directly on research described in Chapters 1, 2, and 3.

1. The Relationship Between Giving and Income. In absolute terms, people with higher incomes give more. This is true both of religious giving and of total giving to both religious and secular organizations. In relative terms— giving as a percentage of income—there is an important complexity that often is overlooked. The conventional wisdom is that people with higher incomes give away proportionately less of it than people with lower incomes, but the research on philanthropic giving in general shows that this is true only if nongivers are excluded from the comparison. This is because people with lower incomes are much more likely to give zero than are people with higher incomes. If such nongivers are included in the comparison, the relationship between income and giving as a percentage of income is either flat or moderately positive; it definitely is not negative. If nongivers are excluded, the relationship is U-shaped, with the lowest-income givers giving away a greater proportion of their income than either middle- or high-income givers. That is, among those who give more than nothing, giving as a percentage of income declines as one moves from the bottom to the middle of the income distribution, and then it rises again as one moves nearer the top of the income distribution. This complexity means that the commonly reported negative relationship between income and religious giving as a proportion of income gives a very partial view of the phenomenon because it usually is based on samples and analyses that include only givers. Because a very different picture emerges when nongivers are included, one should *not* conclude that the less well off are, in general, more generous than the better off (Schervish and Havens 1995).

Although it rarely is, Avner Ben-Ner (1997) has pointed out that this cross-sectional relationship between giving and income should be connected to another basic finding: Giving as a percentage of income has declined over time. Because the broad historical trend is for American households to have higher real incomes over time, this historical trend is another aspect of the finding described in the previous paragraph: Among those who give, religious giving does not keep pace with increases in disposable income.

2. The Relationship Between Giving and Involvement. The relationship between religious giving and involvement in religious organizations is unambiguously positive. Giving is almost always part of a broader involvement with organizations. This is true among the wealthy as much as among the nonwealthy, and it is true for secular giving as well as for religious giving

(Ostrower 1995; Schervish and Havens 1997). This means that people do not, in general, trade off donating time with donating money. The same people who commit the most time to an organization also give the most money to it. Giving is an aspect of—not a substitute for—involvement, and it probably should never be considered in isolation. In this light, a congregation's or denomination's "financial" crisis may be more appropriately understood as an "involvement" crisis. More broadly, the financial aspects of organizations can be seen as windows into deeper and more fundamental dynamics.

Relatedly, religious giving, like secular giving, is very heavily concentrated among a relatively small proportion of those connected to the organization. Approximately three quarters of a typical congregation's resources come from approximately one quarter of the people. Chapter 4 shows why this is so.

3. Giving and Pledging. Planned giving—pledging to give a certain amount over the next year—is correlated with higher levels of giving. Congregations that do not institutionalize planned giving but instead rely on individuals' week-by-week decisions to give gather fewer per capita resources from their congregants. It is not clear, however, that pledging should be considered a cause of higher giving that can be abstracted from its larger context to generate higher levels of giving in new settings. Rather, this result begins to point to one of the larger themes I will highlight below: Giving patterns are inextricably bound up with a whole set of denominational and congregational practices (one of which is pledging) that constitute living religious traditions.

4. Denominational Differences in Individual Giving. There are substantial differences across denominations and religious traditions in both absolute and relative levels of individual giving. Two findings from this body of work shed light on these differences. First, denominational differences are generated almost entirely by the giving of the most committed members within each denomination. These differences emerge only in the top quintile of givers in each denomination. That is, the most committed Catholics give less than the most committed Presbyterians, who give less than the most committed Pentecostals. There are few substantial denominational giving differences among the bottom 80 percent of givers.

Second, attempts to explain these denominational differences in terms of either individual or congregational characteristics are not successful. Almost nothing that appears to be correlated with denominational differences in giving patterns (e.g., conservative theology, congregational size) consistently maintains its explanatory force when we turn to explaining congregational differences within denominations. This is a clue that true causal effects have not been identified. At the same time, factors strongly correlated with congregational differences *within* denominations (e.g., income levels, pledging practices) do not explain denominational differences in giving.

There is one possible exception to this generalization that denominational differences are not reducible to individual and congregational characteristics. I refer to the Hoge et al. finding that "with the adoption of certain Protestant characteristics, most [i.e., more than 80 percent] of the Catholic-Protestant gap [in per capita giving] might be closed" (Hoge et al. 1996:96). Close inspection of this result, however, points to a different conclusion. Protestant-Catholic differences in the demographic characteristics of members (income, education, age) explain none of the gap in giving. Similarly, Protestant-Catholic differences in either member attitudes about their churches or in the stewardship programming of churches explain none of the gap. Other congregational characteristics—size, number of programs offered, and level of debt—have a small impact on the gap in Protestant-Catholic giving. The only factor that "explains" a sizable portion of the gap between Protestant giving and Catholic giving is a theological factor—"attitudes about who can be saved and about the primary duty of Christians" (Hoge et al. 1996:96). I take these results to mean that Catholic giving would be more like Protestant giving if Catholic religious tradition was more Protestant. In this light, the statistical finding that upward of 80 percent of the giving gap is explained by individual and congregational characteristics does not seem an exception to the generalization that denominational differences are not reducible to individual or congregational characteristics.

In my view, the inability to reduce denominational differences to differences in congregational practice or individual characteristics is a very important finding. It is important because it points to the conclusion that denominational giving patterns are fundamentally connected to the religious and institutional practices that make denominations what they are. To say this another way, the inability to explain denominational giving differences by abstracting individual or congregational characteristics (size, pledging, income level, theological content) out of their institutional context suggests that giving patterns are part of the institutionalized religious practices and traditions near the core of denominational identities. In line with this idea, Chapter 5 documents systematic differences among four congregations in what religious giving *means* to people. How a denomination organizes individual giving is part of what and who that denomination *is* as a religious tradition. Attempting to institute tithing, for example, in a denomination for which giving to one's congregation is only one of many possible ways to express faithfulness, generosity, and altruism, may risk altering the core identity of that tradition.

5. Historical Trends. The only well-established individual-level decline in recent decades is in giving as a percentage of income. As described above, this trend should be seen as part of the same phenomenon as the fact that, among those who give more than nothing, giving as a percentage of income decreases as income increases. In absolute terms, by contrast, per capita religious giving among church members has in fact outpaced inflation in recent decades.

6. Giving Among African Americans. Chapter 3 suggests that the basic dynamics of religious giving are the same in predominantly black churches as they are in predominantly white churches. That is, giving levels are highly and positively correlated with income and involvement, and there are denominational differences in cultures of giving that are not unlike the denominational differences observed among predominantly white denominations.

Religion and Economic Life

Chapter 8 documents that individuals are not, in general, helped by churches and clergy when it comes to thinking about their larger economic lives. With respect to economic behavior in general, there are few, if any, differences between active church attenders and nonattenders in the way people think about work, experience work, or behave at work. It seems that the disjunction between faith and money is broader than the pragmatic issue of how much people put in offering plates.

Congregational Resource Allocation

Congregations spend proportionally more of their money supporting their local operations than in the 1950s heyday of national denominations. Hoge et al. (1996:15) say that, "In the mid-1990s, an average of 10 to 15 percent of all contributions are being spent on missions outside the local church, whereas in the 1950s, the figure was roughly twice as high." This trend, however, should be seen in the context of three other observations.

First, there have been previous periods—in particular from the early 1920s to the late 1930s—of substantial decline in the proportion of congregational resources passed on to denominations. The twentieth-century high point in benevolent spending by congregations appears to have been in 1920, a short-term effect of the large-scale fund-raising drives immediately following World War I. Fahs (1929) reports that congregations spent an average of 35 percent on "benevolences" in 1920, declining to 22 percent in 1927. According to the 1936 U.S. census of religious bodies, by the middle of the 1930s congregations were spending only 13.6 percent of their resources on other than local operations.

Second, although the proportion of total giving that is passed on to denominations has declined since the 1950s, the absolute amount of per capita giving to denominations has *not* declined. This means that the proportion going to denominations has declined because the amount given to denominations *has not increased at the same rate* as giving for local congregational operations.

Third, it is important to note that analyses of these trends largely ignore the historical shift from an era in which individuals gave directly to national organizations, primarily mission societies, to an era in which such giving was largely channeled through congregations. The "denominationalization" of missions and other national agencies, and the creation of unified denominational budgets—both developments of turn-of-the-century decades—changed the institutional and financial relations between congregations and denominations.

In this context, the post-1950s decline in congregational support of denominations seems both less significant and less unprecedented. Indeed, it may be that asking, "Why the decline in denominational support?" misdirects attention from another story: the *increase* in per capita spending on congregations' local operations.

Historicizing Religious Financing

Both the infrastructure of religious financing and the language used to understand it are historically variable, as Chapters 6 and 7 make clear. The "stewardship" and "systematic benevolence" regimes we live under now—voluntary giving to congregations that then funnel money to other enterprises—emerged at the end of the nineteenth and the beginning of the twentieth centuries. Although the language of stewardship is the only theological language widely used today to discuss money and resources in religious organizations, the exact meanings attached to "stewardship" have varied over time and across religious settings. Currently, there is disagreement about whether or not the language of stewardship adequately communicates religious meanings concerning money.

Explaining Lower Levels of Catholic Giving

As reported in Chapter 1, it now is possible to rule out with confidence several commonly offered explanations for the well-established finding that Catholic per capita giving is substantially lower than Protestant giving. This difference is *not* caused by any of the following: (1) Catholics are angrier with church leaders; (2) Catholics give more to nonparish Catholic causes and organizations; (3) Catholics are more likely to send their children to parochial schools; (4) Catholic churches are less democratic; or (5) Catholics believe that their churches are less in need of money. The true effect of congregational size on Protestant-Catholic differences in giving remains unclear. Broadly, the Catholic-versus-Protestant difference in giving appears to be a special case of the larger phenomenon to which I already have pointed: Giving differences are one aspect of deeper institutionalized differences in religious culture and practice.

Management Skills of Leaders

With respect to obtaining and managing material resources, Chapter 11 documents the fact that there are serious shortcomings in knowledge, skill, and will among those who lead religious organizations. It is not uncommon for clergy and other leaders not to know how to develop a budget, oversee spending, seek a grant, manage an endowment, invest funds, manage physical plants, and so on. Seminaries do not, in general, require students to learn the administrative skills that might be of use to those expected to lead congregations and other religious organizations.

This is not simply a matter of skill deficit. There also appears to be a tendency among clergy to consciously separate religious, spiritual, and pastoral authority and responsibilities from practical, financial, and administrative authority and responsibilities. This combination—lack of administrative skill plus a belief, apparently common among clergy, that one's proper professional role is pastoral rather than administrative—increases the likelihood that the resources of religious organizations will be poorly managed, a possibility also suggested by results reported in Chapter 10.

Aggregate Numbers

Although none of these chapters address this issue directly, it is important to note that there still is huge uncertainty in estimates of the aggregate level of resources available to religious organizations. Ronsvalle and Ronsvalle

(1995:45-46) compare three estimates of aggregate giving to religion. Summing giving to the 28 denominations for which good data exist in 1993 yields a total of $18.5 billion given in that year. This figure clearly understates the total amount of giving to religion, since it includes only giving to denominationally affiliated congregations, and several major denominations are excluded from this summation.

Another estimate comes from the Independent Sector's surveys of individuals about their giving. In their 1993 survey, the average household contribution to religion was $402. Multiplying that figure by the number of households in the United States yields an estimate of $39 billion given to religion in 1993 (Hodgkinson and Weitzman 1994). This number would include giving to all religious organizations, not just congregations.

Yet a third estimate comes from the American Association of Fund-Raising Counsel, a group of professional fund-raising organizations. They combine individual-level survey data with data from tax returns and from surveys of organizations to estimate the total amount given to religion from all sources—not just from individuals. Their estimate for 1993 was $56.3 billion (Kaplan 1995).

What can we conclude from these estimates? It seems that the best we can say is that aggregate giving to religion from individuals in 1993 probably was between $18.5 billion and $39 billion, and that overall giving to religion, from all sources, probably was between $39 billion and $56.3 billion. The most important conclusion, however, is probably the huge degree of uncertainty that still exists regarding the total amount of money given to American religion in any given year. We should be sobered by the prospect that estimates of the total amount of giving to religion in the United States could be off by *billions* of dollars, yet we are not yet in a position to provide more precision.[1]

CROSSCUTTING THEMES

Denominational Differences

Denominational differences in religious giving represent institutional differences that are not reducible to individual-level, rational calculations. Several findings point to the general conclusion that denominational variations in religious giving represent variations in the institutionalized practices by

---

1 See Schervish and Havens (1998) for the most recent evidence on this subject.

which congregations gather resources. This implies that individual giving to religion is in some respects quite unlike purchasing a product, and attempts to understand it as such will mislead rather than inform. If religious giving was fundamentally like purchasing a product, people should give more when congregations provide more (or better) programming, and they should give more when their rational decision-making faculties are appealed to via stewardship programs and emphases. Neither of these appears to be the case. This body of work suggests that religious giving does not, in general, respond either to increased programming or to explicit appeals for individuals to rethink their giving levels. There appear to be few, if any, nonfundamental, nontheological, noncultural, noninstitutional ways to change giving patterns.

Instead, it seems that significant change in religious giving patterns in a given congregation or denomination is likely only via institutional change, by which I mean reconfiguring religious and ritual practices so that giving has a different place and meaning than it did before. The difference between denominations with higher and lower levels of per capita giving is that giving is incorporated in a different way into collective religious practice. If giving patterns are an aspect of the collective religious practice that makes a denomination a distinct religious tradition, then changing giving patterns means changing the tradition. There appears to be no way to make Lutheran or Presbyterian per capita giving rise to the level of Mormon or Seventh-day Adventist giving without making Presbyterian and Lutheran religious traditions into something other than what they currently are. Saying to a religious organization, "institutionalize a pledge system" or "train people to tithe" or "create an endowment" may be tantamount to saying, "change your religious tradition."

Theology and Money

Understanding the relationship between theology and money in religious organizations requires distinguishing between theology as doctrine or belief and theology as institutionalized practice. Running throughout these chapters is the theme that theology—understood as self-conscious, articulated, theological reasoning or God-talk—is very much uncoupled from resource management. Quantitatively, differences in the content of individuals' religious beliefs have inconsistent and difficult to interpret effects on religious giving and, more generally, on the ways people think and act economically. Qualitatively, several researchers highlight the striking absence of explicit theological considerations as important factors in congregational decision making about both raising and using money.

If, however, we shift our attention to what might be called institutionalized theology—theological ideas that may not be self-consciously held by anyone in a congregation but that are institutionalized in congregational practices of religious organizations—then theology is absolutely fundamental to the ways that religious organizations seek and use resources. From this perspective, differences in institutionalized practices (pledging, tithing, financial connections between congregations and denominations, developing endowments, etc.) represent *theological* differences. The general conclusion here is that theological differences matter very much to the handling of material resources in religious organizations, but only to the extent that they are institutionalized.

Financing National Denominations

The current financial woes of some national denominations do not represent the dawn of an unprecedented, "postmodern" era in American religion. It is important to see that strong and well-supported national denominational structures were a relatively recent achievement in American organized religion. We perhaps are moving toward a situation that will resemble the pre-World-War-I organizational conditions in American religion more than it will resemble the post-World War II heyday of national denominations, but there is little reason to think that we are entering an unprecedented historical situation—in regard to financing—that is qualitatively different from anything that has come before. The rise and fall of strong, relatively centralized national denominations is part and parcel of similar historical patterns among both government and business organizations. The current organizational fad is toward local control, and it is important to place current organizational trends in American religion in the context of this larger cultural pattern.

It is informative in this regard to note the causal factors that Fahs (1929) considered as possible explanations for the 1920s decline in benevolent spending and increase in the proportion of funds congregations spent locally. They are surprisingly similar to contemporary explanations commonly offered for the more recent decline in the extent to which congregations support denominations financially. Among the possible causal factors Fahs considered in 1929 were (1) that churches were spending less on benevolences because local expenses (in the form of interest payments on debt) had increased; (2) that denominational officials (because of the 1920s trend toward unifying denominational budgets) were out of touch with the concerns of people in the pews; and (3) that there was increased competition for congregational funds from "mission societies and agencies strongly conservative theologically, but not related directly to the denominations" (p. 67). Today, some suggest that increased health insurance and energy costs rather than indebtedness increase local operating costs for congregations, argue that "liberal" national programs rather than unified budgets have alienated laity, and posit a postmodern pattern by which congregations consider denominations to be only one of many parachurch organizations to which they might contribute. That these same basic factors were believed to underlie a previous shift toward congregations spending more of their funds on local operations is something worth pondering.

Where Is the Crisis?

Perceptions of crisis in the financing of American religion are strongest among those who compare the present to the unusually flush years of the 1950s. I am struck by the fact that black church leaders do not seem to experience the present financial state of African American churches as qualitatively different from that of the past. I think this is because black church leaders did not experience a period of unusual plenty against which the present looks bad. There is no bust unless one first has a boom.

This suggests that much of the present sense of financial crisis elsewhere in American religion may be because of the inability to continue national programs and organizations that were overbuilt in a time of unusual plenty. It is important, however, to note that it was the post-World War II time of plenty that was anomalous. It may be helpful to extend our historical horizon so that the visual image of change regarding the financial health of American religion looks more like an inverted "U" than a downward sloping straight line. That is, the twentieth-century story of national denominational organizations is not a story of linear decline but a story of a period of relative scarcity followed by a time of plenty followed by another period of relative scarcity. Referring to concrete religious organizations, this "inverted U" narrative apparently applies not only to the financial health of some national denominations, but also to Catholic schools and Jewish philanthropic organizations (see Chapter 12 of this volume; Adelson 1997).

That said, the crisis is real from the perspective of leaders of religious organizations that are experiencing decline and resource scarcity. Pointing out that such crisis is not universal, and not historically unprecedented, may help give leaders a sense of perspective, but it will not provide the practical help needed to guide their struggling organizations. Perhaps the best way to summarize the findings of this work regarding the presence or absence of crisis is this: "Crisis" does not characterize American religion as a whole, nor does it characterize the era in which we live. The current financial crisis is

located in certain specific organizations, and it is best understood as an uncertainty among leaders about how responsibly and faithfully to guide specific religious organizations into an unstable future.

Financial Crisis as Involvement Crisis

Financial crisis may be better understood as involvement crisis. A point
made earlier is worth elaborating here. Financial crises in voluntary organizations such as churches may often be, in essence, involvement crises. The
fact that per capita religious giving in absolute terms actually has *increased*
over time is relevant here. It suggests that, in the major denominations that
have seen significant membership decline in conjunction with stable or even
increased giving from those who remain, labeling the current situation a
"financial crisis" represents a major misdiagnosis. It seems likely that financial stress is a symptom of something more fundamental.

NORMATIVE ISSUES

Religious Organizations and Their Environments

The first set of normative questions involves interactions between religious organizations and their institutional environments. The future of congregations and other religious organizations will be partly shaped by the
institutions, professions, and traditions from which they draw models, analo-
gies, and other guides for action. In the present context, an important decision faced by many religious organizations is whether or not to turn to the
larger nonprofit world and its ways of understanding, seeking, and managing
material resources. This decision has normative as well as empirical dimensions. For example, results reported in Chapters 16 and 17 raise the question
of whether or not small religious nonprofit organizations ought to adopt
standard accounting practices or board structures. This question is not ex-
haustively answered by the empirical fact that such change is likely to increase their ability to secure either government or foundation funding. The
decision also has a normative dimension that is not reducible to the practical
dimension of which course of action will generate the most money.

Among the relevant normative questions here are these: To what extent
should religious organizations orient themselves more to the secular nonprofit world when it comes to seeking and maintaining material resources,
and to what extent should they maintain their distance? Which practices

commonly used in the secular nonprofit world would be appropriately adopted by those who run religious organizations, and which ones should be avoided? Should ministers who lead congregations think of themselves as, at least in part, executive directors of nonprofit organizations? Should congregational boards of elders (or the equivalent) model themselves after nonprofit boards of directors? Should religious organizations adopt professional fund-raising models, techniques, and vocabularies? Empirical research can be informative about some of the consequences of choosing one path or the other, but it cannot be the sole guide for deciding the desirability of one path or the other.

Assessing Potential Changes

A second set of normative questions involves how to assess changing religious practices concerning resources. I argued above that giving patterns and resource management practices are one aspect of the religious practices and traditions that make denominations what they are. Empirically, this suggests that changing these practices will rarely be easy, even in the presence of solid knowledge implying that a certain change will lead to more resources. Normatively, this raises a set of questions: Should religious organizations change their religious practices and traditions in order to obtain resources? How would one assess whether a particular practice regarding resources is essential to or merely a peripheral aspect of a religious tradition? How would one assess whether or not a proposed new practice runs counter to a religious tradition's core identity?

Reasons for Giving

A third normative issue concerns the articulation of reasons for giving. I argued above that a key to understanding giving practices is understanding the ways in which they become institutionalized, by which I mean the ways in which they become relatively automatic, habitual, and unself-consciously part of what it means to be involved in a congregation. From this perspective, it seems unlikely that encouraging individuals to articulate theological motives and reasons for giving will have pragmatic payoffs in terms of increased or more regular giving. It might be, of course, that such articulation is a desirable end in itself. Still, a normative question is raised: Should religious leaders encourage individuals to develop and articulate theological reasons for giving? If so, why?

DIRECTIONS FOR FUTURE RESEARCH

This volume presents a snapshot of what is known about financing American religion circa 1998. It also, of course, reveals more clearly what is not yet known. There is more work to be done in this arena, and I conclude by suggesting several directions that seem particularly in need of additional work.

First, future work should focus on the cultural and institutional differences among religious traditions as the most likely source of denominational variation in giving patterns. It seems that we know almost all there is to know about individual-level determinants of giving *within* specific institutional contexts. We still do not fully understand, however, how different institutional contexts—represented by denominational traditions but not only by denominational traditions—came to be, and how giving and financing and, more generally, money, are embedded within those different complexes of practices and traditions. Sorting this out will require historical and comparative work in which religious traditions—coherent sets of institutionalized practice—are the primary units of analysis rather than individuals or congregations.

This recommendation implies expanding the scope of study to encompass more variation than exists simply among Christian traditions. Important variation in religious culture and institutionalized practice is not captured by an exclusive focus on denominational differences. Other dimensions of variation might include ethnicity and region, as well as the broad spectrum of non-Christian traditions, and all of these can be studied historically as well as cross-sectionally. Placing Christian financial practices in a context enlarged in this way might very well spark newly creative thinking about the range of available possibilities.

Second, future work should expand the study of congregational financing beyond individual giving. We now know much about individual giving to congregations, but it seems that the overall mix of financial resources available to congregations might be changing in ways that will enhance the importance of resources other than individual donations. This possibility raises several important questions: What are the consequences of different mixes of resource streams for congregations? What is likely to happen if a congregation gathers more resources from government or foundation grants? From a newly created endowment? From fees charged for services delivered? Kirsten Grønbjerg (1993) has addressed these questions for other organizational populations; addressing them for congregations may be very worthwhile.

Third, future work should expand the study of giving beyond congregations. As above, the focus to date on individual giving to congregations means that relatively little attention has been paid to individual giving to other sorts of religious organizations. How do dynamics of individual giving to congregations and other face-to-face voluntary associations differ from the dynamics of giving to religious organizations that are not of this sort? Research focused on sorting out how the dynamics of giving differ with respect to different sorts of target organizations—and different ways in which individuals relate to those organizations—would be able to address this question.

Fourth, future work should focus on the spending and cost side of the financing issue. We now know much more about how congregations and other religious organizations *get* their material resources than we know about how they *spend* them. There is good reason to think that issues of cost and liability have as much—perhaps more—of an effect on religious organizations' overall financing challenges than do issues of giving and fund-raising. It may be worth pursuing research that focuses more directly on the debit side of religious financing.

Fifth, future work should focus on the legal and regulatory framework affecting resource streams of religious organizations (see Bassett 1997 for an example of work along this line). A guiding question here might be: To what extent are the resource issues faced by religious organizations shaped by the regulatory environment and thereby subject to change in response to changes in that environment? It is likely that regulations governing income tax reporting, property tax exemptions, clergy IRS status, inherited wealth, liability, government support of congregation-based social services, and so on, fundamentally shape the material resources available to religious organizations in ways that we do not yet fully understand. Furthermore, in line with the point made in the previous paragraph, the regulatory environment also affects how religious organizations *spend* their money as much as, perhaps more than, it affects how religious organizations *gather* resources. Cross-national comparisons, by observing a wider range of regulatory settings in which religion is embedded, could be very informative in this regard.

Relatedly, recent years have seen a raised consciousness in the nonprofit and policy worlds about religion and religious organizations, and it seems a real possibility that foundations and state governments will seek to channel social service money through congregations and other religious organizations at an unprecedented level. This prospect raises a set of very important empirical and normative questions about the activities such money will be allowed to support and the ways in which religious organizations will have to structure themselves and their activities in order to receive such support.

In this context, future research might address the question: What consequences would the potential increased availability of foundation and government funds have on religious organizations?

Sixth, future work should place research on the financing of religious organizations more explicitly in the context of resource issues facing nonprofit organizations in general. Grønbjerg (1997), for example, has pointed out that fund-raising is increasingly professionalized, and there is a shift in the nonprofit world from general institutional support to program-specific support. Future research might investigate the practical and theological consequences of these broader trends for religious organizations.

More generally, this body of work makes progress on but does not completely settle the question of the extent to which religious organizations are different from their secular counterparts in securing, managing, and using material resources. For example, do religious or congregation-based social service organizations use resources more or less efficiently and effectively than secular social service organizations? What is the relative importance of functional field of operation (e.g., social service delivery vs. education) and religious versus secular auspices in determining organizational behavior? Until we know more about how religious organizations are similar to and different from secular voluntary organizations regarding financing and other issues, it will be difficult to be confident about distinguishing between the challenges that leaders can do something about and the challenges that are less amenable to change from within any particular organization. There is some work that begins to address this question (see, for example, Weisbrod 1998, Mauser 1998, and Chapters 15 and 16 of this volume), but much more is needed.

Seventh, future work should address questions of inequality within denominations and congregations. There is huge variation in both income and wealth among religious organizations. To give just one example, from Chapter 10, the total wealth held by the relatively few Presbyterian congregations with large endowments is on the order of half a billion dollars. To date, research on financing American religion has tended to focus on average and aggregate levels of resources available to the universe of religious organizations. Perhaps it would be helpful to shift the focus from averages to the variation around those averages. Beginning with the observation that there is huge wealth already existing within at least some (probably most) denominations, the idea here is that it might be fruitful to shift the guiding question from, How might more resources be brought *into* the religious sphere? to, How might the tremendous resources already existing *within* the religious sphere be more efficiently and effectively used?

It is clear, for example, that some congregations that are far from vital religious communities are able to survive only because they are able to draw from savings accounts, endowments, or income from the sale or lease of property. How much "religious wealth" is used in this way? How might congregations in this situation be helped to think creatively about how to use their resources? Relatedly, it is clear that some redistribution of wealth occurs within denominations—better-off congregations give money either directly to struggling congregations or to denominational agencies that then support struggling congregations. Research has not yet attended to this aspect of religious resources. To what extent does this sort of redistribution occur? What happens when struggling congregations receive this sort of assistance?

Eighth, future work should expand the scope of study to include the world of entrepreneurial religion. When I tell people that I have been working on the financing of American religion, the most common response is something like, "So, how much do those televangelists get?" Although televangelism was extensively studied in the 1980s, this response points, I think, to an area that has not yet received sufficient attention: the financing of religious activity that does not run through traditional congregations affiliated with historic denominations. The work described in Chapter 14, on parachurch organizations, is a start, but there is more to know. How are nondenominational megachurches financed? What about new religious movements? More generally (and perhaps more significantly), is the evangelical world overbuilding now in much the same way that the "mainline" overbuilt in the 1950s?

Ninth, there is more to learn about organizational size. Whether an organization is large or small profoundly affects many things. This appears to be true for both secular and religious organizations, and it appears to be true for virtually every kind of religious organization—from congregations to seminaries to parachurch organizations. That is, for each type of religious organization, it seems true that small ones are qualitatively different from large ones. So far, size has been systematically considered in this body of work only with respect to its possible effects on individual giving to congregations, and the results on that score are ambiguous. We still do not know whether large congregations lead people to give less.

Additional work focused on the consequences of organizational size therefore is in order. In addition to trying to nail down the effect of size on individual giving to congregations, perhaps it also would be valuable to broaden the scope of attention and examine how size affects the way resources are used in different types of religious organizations. Guiding questions here might be, At a given level of per capita giving, how do resource issues faced by congregations change as size increases? Are there identifiable economies of scale? What are the consequences of growth for seminaries, parachurch organizations, congregations?

CONCLUSION

The Lilly Endowment's Financing of American Religion initiative clearly has succeeded in generating new knowledge, and it has called the attention of scholars and practitioners to the issue of religious organizations and their resources. I trust that this volume serves to communicate the current state of our knowledge on this important topic, and I hope that it will help inspire others to expand our knowledge still further. If this volume is truly effective, it soon will be transcended by the next wave of work on this topic.

REFERENCES

Adelson, Evan. 1997. "The Good, The Bad and The Ugly: Moral Behavior, Community Coercion and Philanthropic Practice." Unpublished manuscript, Department of Sociology, University of California, San Diego.

Bassett, William. 1997. *Religious Organizations and the Law*. New York: Clark, Boardman, Callahan.

Ben-Ner, Avner. 1997. "General Comments on the 'Financing of American Religion' Project: Patterns of Giving." Unpublished manuscript, University of Minnesota, Minneapolis.

Fahs, Charles. 1929. *Trends in Protestant Giving: A Study of Church Finance in the United States*. New York: Institute of Social and Religious Research.

Grønbjerg, Kirsten. 1993. *Understanding Nonprofit Funding: Managing Revenues in Social Services and Community Development Organizations*. San Francisco: Jossey-Bass.

————. 1997. "Lilly Endowment Financing American Religion Project. Evaluator's Assessment: Key Conceptual Issues, Lessons Learned, and Future Research." Unpublished manuscript, Indiana University, Bloomington.

Hodgkinson, Virginia A., and Murray S. Weitzman. 1994. *Giving and Volunteering in the United States*. Washington, DC: Independent Sector.

Hoge, Dean R., Charles Zech, Patrick McNamara, and Michael J. Donahue. 1996. *Money Matters: Personal Giving in American Churches*. Louisville, KY: Westminster John Knox.

Kaplan, Ann E. 1995. *Giving USA 1995*. New York: American Association of Fund-Raising Counsel Trust for Philanthropy.

Mauser, Elizabeth. 1998. "The Importance of Organizational Form: Parent Perceptions Versus Reality in the Day Care Industry." Pp. 124-133 in *Private Action and the Public Good*, edited by Walter W. Powell and Elisabeth S. Clemens. New Haven, CT: Yale University Press.

Ostrower, Francie. 1995. *Why the Wealthy Give: The Culture of Elite Philanthropy*. Princeton, NJ: Princeton University Press.

Ronsvalle, John, and Sylvia Ronsvalle. 1995. *The State of Church Giving Through 1993*. Champaign, IL: empty tomb, inc.

Schervish, Paul G., and John J. Havens. 1995. "Do the Poor Pay More? Is the U-Shaped Curve Correct?" *Nonprofit and Voluntary Sector Quarterly* 24:79-90.

———. 1997. "Social Participation and Charitable Giving: A Multivariate Analysis." *Voluntas* 8:235-260.

———. 1998. "Embarking on a Republic of Benevolence? New Survey Findings on Charitable Giving." *Nonprofit and Voluntary Sector Quarterly* 27: 237-242.

Weisbrod, Burton A. 1998. "Institutional Form and Organizational Behavior." Pp. 69-84 in *Private Action and the Public Good*, edited by Walter W. Powell and Elisabeth S. Clemens. New Haven, CT: Yale University Press.

Index

About the Authors

Ellen J. Benjamin is Assistant Professor in the School for New Learning at DePaul University, in Chicago, Illinois, where she teaches and conducts research on nonprofit management and philanthropy. Her nonprofit experience includes 15 years directing grantmaking institutions, as well as extensive hands-on work with social service and advocacy organizations as a founder, employee, trustee, and volunteer.

Mark Chaves is Associate Professor of Sociology at the University of Arizona. He recently published *Ordaining Women: Culture and Conflict in Religious Organizations* (1997). Currently, he is working on the National Congregations Study, a national survey of religious congregations generated from the 1998 General Social Survey.

Walter V. Collier, a social scientist and policy analyst, has worked as a researcher in the public, business, and voluntary sectors for over 25 years. He is president of Collier & Associates, a management information and research consultant firm in Oak Bluffs, Massachusetts.

Daniel Conway is Director of Stewardship and Development for the Archdiocese of Chicago, the second largest Roman Catholic diocese in the United States. He also serves as Director of the National Catholic Stewardship Council's Summer Institute for Stewardship and Development.

Michael J. Donahue is a Catholic layman and independent research consultant living in Minneapolis, Minnesota. In addition to working with denominations in the financing study on which Chapter 1 is based, he also held a postdoctoral fellowship in psychology of religion at Brigham Young University (1981-1983), and he is developing survey instruments for the Seventh-day Adventist Church.

Kirsten A. Grønbjerg is Professor and Associate Dean for Academic Affairs in the School of Public and Environmental Affairs at Indiana University, Bloomington, and Adjunct Professor of Philanthropic Studies at the Center on Philanthropy at Indiana University. Her interests focus on the structure of public and nonprofit human service systems, and her most recent book is *Understanding Nonprofit Funding: Managing Revenues in Social Services and Community Development Organizations* (1993).

Joseph Claude Harris works as comptroller for the St. Vincent de Paul Society, Seattle. He is the author of *The Cost of Catholic Parishes and Schools* (1996).

Virginia Hodgkinson is Research Professor of Public Policy at the Center for the Study of Voluntary Organizations and Service, Georgetown Public Policy Institute, Georgetown University. Formerly she was Vice President for Research at Independent Sector. Her latest books are *Nonprofit Almanac: Dimensions of the Independent Sector, 1996-1997* (1996) and *Care and Community in Modern Society: Passing on the Tradition of Service to Future Generations* (1995).

Dean R. Hoge is Professor of Sociology at Catholic University of America, Washington, D.C. His most recent coauthored books are *Vanishing Boundaries: The Religion of Mainline Protestant Baby Boomers* (1994) and *Money Matters: Personal Giving in American Churches* (1996).

James Hudnut-Beumler is Professor of Religion and Culture at Columbia Theological Seminary in Decatur, Georgia. Specializing in contemporary American religious history, he is author of *Looking for God in the Suburbs: The Religion of the American Dream and Its Critics, 1945-1965* (1994).

Laurence R. Iannaccone is Professor of Economics at Santa Clara University. His studies of religion have appeared in numerous books and journals, including *American Economic Review, American Journal of Sociology, Journal* *of Political Economy, Journal for the Scientific Study of Religion,* and *Social Forces.* He is writing a book on the economics of religion.

Robert Wood Lynn is an independent teacher and researcher. He has served as a Protestant minister, a seminary dean, and a foundation staff member.

Patrick McNamara is Professor of Sociology at the University of New Mexico. He is coauthor of *Money Matters: Personal Giving in American Churches* (1996) and *Plain Talk About Churches and Money* (1997). He is currently at work on a book about churches with outstanding stewardship programs.

Loren B. Mead is an ordained Episcopal priest and the author of *The Once and Future Church: Transforming Congregations for the Future,* and *Five Challenges for the Once and Future Church* (1996). His most recent book, *Financial Meltdown in the Mainline?* (forthcoming) is on the financial and spiritual dilemmas of church financing.

Sharon L. Miller is a doctoral candidate in sociology at the University of Notre Dame and Visiting Assistant Professor at Hope College in Holland, Michigan. Her research interests include the financing of churches and religious bodies and the intersection of gender and religion.

John M. Mulder is President and Professor of Historical Theology at Louisville Presbyterian Theological Seminary. With Milton J. Coalter and Louis B. Weeks, he coauthored *Vital Signs: The Promise of Mainstream Protestantism* (1996) and collaborated on the seven-volume study of American Presbyterianism in the twentieth century, *The Presbyterian Presence* (1990).

Sheila Nelson is Assistant Professor of Sociology at the College of St. Benedict/St. John's University in Collegeville, Minnesota. Her research interests include inner-city Catholic schools, religiously sponsored social service organizations, and organizational change among American religious congregations of women.

Michael O'Neill is Professor and Director of the Institute for Nonprofit Organization Management at the University of San Francisco. He is the author or coauthor of several books on the nonprofit sector, including *The Third America* (1989), *Educating Managers of Nonprofit Organizations* (1988), *Ethics in Nonprofit Management* (1990), *Hispanics and the Nonprofit Sector* (1991), *Women and Power in the Nonprofit Sector* (1994), and *Nonprofit*

Management Education: U.S. and World Perspectives (1998). He is president of the Association for Research on Nonprofit Organizations and Voluntary Action (ARNOVA).

Calvin O. Pressley, ordained in the United Methodist Church, has been a pastor and organizer for many years in the African American community. He is currently the executive director of the Institute of Church Administration and Management at the Interdenominational Theological Center in Atlanta, Georgia.

John Ronsvalle and Sylvia Ronsvalle serve through empty tomb, inc., a research and service organization based in Champaign, Illinois. They are exploring, with selected congregations, how to reverse negative giving trends. The working title of their next book is *From Loneliness to Freedom: Small Groups and Money.*

Anthony Ruger is Research Fellow at the Center for the Study of Theological Education at Auburn Theological Seminary. He has consulted widely with religious organizations on financial and strategic matters. From 1988 to 1998 he served as treasurer of the Association of Theological Schools in the U.S. and Canada.

Robert Wuthnow is Gerhard R. Andlinger Professor of Sociology and Director of the Center for the Study of American Religion at Princeton University. His most recent books are *After Heaven: Spirituality in America Since the 1950s* (1998) and *Loose Connections: Joining Together in America's Fragmented Communities* (1998).

Charles Zech is Professor of Economics at Villanova University. He has authored or coauthored over 50 articles and books, including *The Mainline Church's Funding Crisis* (1995), *Money Matters: Personal Giving in American Churches* (1996), and *Plain Talk About Churches and Money* (1997).